Michael Grant has been successively Chancellor's medallist
and Fellow of Trinity College, Cambridge, Professor of
Humanity at Edinburgh University, first Vice-Chancellor
of Khartoum University, and President and Vice-Chancellor
of the Queen's University of Belfast. Until 1966 he was
President of the Virgil Society. He has also translated
Tacitus' *Annals of Imperial Rome*, Cicero's *Selected Works*,
Selected Political Speeches and philosophical essays (*On
the Good Life*) for the Penguin Classics; his other books
include *The World of Rome* (1960), *Myths of the Greeks
and Romans* (1962), *The Civilizations of Europe* (1965),
Roman Readings and *Roman Literature* (both available in
Pelicans), *The Climax of Rome* (1968), *The Ancient
Mediterranean*, *Julius Caesar* (1969), *The Ancient
Historians*, *The Roman Forum*, and *Nero* (1970).

MICHAEL GRANT

GLADIATORS

PENGUIN BOOKS

Penguin Books Ltd, Harmondsworth,
Middlesex, England
Penguin Books Australia Ltd, Ringwood,
Victoria, Australia

First published by Weidenfeld & Nicolson 1967
This slightly revised version published in Pelican Books 1971

Made and printed in Great Britain by
Richard Clay (The Chaucer Press) Ltd,
Bungay, Suffolk
Set in Linotype Pilgrim

CONTENTS

ACKNOWLEDGEMENTS

The author and publishers are grateful for permission to quote copyright material from the following books: *Martial's Epigrams,* trans. A. L. Francis and H. F. Tatum (Cambridge University Press); *The Roman Republic, II,* Thomas Rice Holmes (Clarendon Press); *Cicero, Tusc. II,* trans. J. E. King, *Cicero, Att. VII,* trans. E. O. Windstedt, *Dio Cassius, LXVII, LXXIII,* trans. H. B. Foster and E. Cary, *Josephus, Antiquitates Judaicae, XIX,* trans. L. H. Feldman, *Josephus, Bellum Judaicum, VII,* trans. K. St J. Thackeray, *Pliny, Letters X,* trans. W. Melmoth and W.M.L. Hutchinson, *Quintilian, II,* trans. H. E. Butler, *Seneca, Ep. Mor. VII,* trans. R. M. Gummere, *Tertullian, De Spectaculis,* trans. T. R. Glover (Heinemann and Harvard University Press); *The Aeneid of Virgil,* trans. C. Day Lewis (Hogarth Press Ltd, by permission of A. D. Peters Ltd); *The Satires of Juvenal, III, VI, VIII,* trans. R. Humphries, *Persius, VI,* trans. W. S. Merwin (Indiana University Press); *Leisure and Pleasure in Roman Egypt,* J. Lindsay (Frederick Muller Ltd and Messrs Barnes & Noble Inc.); *Apuleius, Metamorphoses, VI, X* and *Suetonius, Caesars,* trans. R. Graves (Penguin Books Ltd, by permission of A. P. Watt & Son); *Petronius, Satyricon,* trans. J. Sullivan, *Plutarch, Crassus,* trans. R. Warner (Penguin Books Ltd, by permission of David Higham Associates); *Daily Life in Ancient Rome,* J. Carcopino, *Ovid, Ars Amatoria,* F. A. Wright, *Roman Life and Manners under the Early Empire,* L. Friedländer, *Sexual Life in Ancient Rome,* O. Kiefer (Routledge & Kegan Paul Ltd); *Roman Art and Architecture,* Sir Mortimer Wheeler (Thames & Hudson Ltd).

8 Acknowledgements

They are also indebted to the following for providing illustrative material : Gabinetto Fotografico Nazionale, Rome; Giraudon, Paris; Galleria Borghese, Rome; Instituto Archeologico Germanico, Rome; The Mansell Collection, London; Museo del Sannio, Benevento; Paul Popper Ltd, London; Oscar Savio; Adolfo Tomeucci; Unione dell'Accademia Americana, Rome.

INTRODUCTION

GLADIATORS became so ingrained in the Roman mind and soul that all manner of strange superstitions proliferated around them. It was believed that the warm blood of a slaughtered gladiator would cure epilepsy. And when newly married women, in accordance with custom, parted their hair with a spear, it brought good luck if this had belonged to a man mortally wounded in the arena. Magical emblems intended to influence the results of gladiatorial combats have been found in amphitheatres, in England and elsewhere. According to the Sicilian astrologer Firmicus Maternus – before he was converted to Christianity – the disaster and death which lay in wait for gladiators could be predetermined by studying the stars : and magical papyri, too, tell of the violent ends to which they were doomed. Moreover, people often dreamt they were gladiators. In the second century AD an expounder of dreams, Artemidorus of Daldis in Asia Minor, suggested that if your dream-opponent was the type of gladiator known as a Thracian, this had a matrimonial significance : it meant you were going to marry a rich, crafty, egotistical woman. He added something easy to believe – that serving for many years in the profession (though few survived to do so) produced a tendency to suffer nightmares.

These are the fringe-products of an institution for which the Romans bear an infinite load of guilt. Of course, they have also contributed a host of wonderful gifts to posterity and to our own civilization. Without these inheritances, many of the finer features of our world would not exist, and this applies alike to government, law, literature, philosophy, art, and material life. It was because of the *pax Romana* that Greek culture was able to survive and pass down the ages. The same peaceful extension of Roman rule enabled Christianity to take root and spread.

But history does not permit peoples to be judged by a simple good or bad mark. Least of all is this possible for the Romans, since their achievements were accompanied and counterbalanced by dreadful savageries, of which none was more horrible than gladiatorial combat. This setting of human beings to kill one another in public, for entertainment, is by far the nastiest blood-sport ever invented.

The brutality which the custom exhibited in so extravagant a form was abundant in many shapes throughout the world of the ancient Romans. It would therefore be a disservice to truth to brush the gladiators aside, or vaguely take refuge in the grandeur that was Rome. The adoption of a realistic attitude about this aspect of *Romanità* is all the more necessary in our own twentieth century. For this, in spite of its many advantages unavailable to the Romans, is one of the extremely few epochs of human history to have achieved cruelty on a scale as numerically lavish as ancient Rome; though the Assyrians and Genghiz Khan and Timur, and English and other slave traders, are competitors.

No amount of explanation can mitigate the savagery. Yet, in various ways, good things came out of even this almost supreme degree of evil. It brought forth countless acts of individual courage of the highest order. It created one of the world's greatest architectural forms. It inspired a number of thoughtful pagans, mostly Greeks or Hellenized orientals but also an occasional Roman, to write down violent protests which stood firm against the overwhelming tide. And the brutal and brutalizing atrocities gave added strength and urgency to the rise of Christianity and to its respect for individual life which, in the end, did away with the gladiators altogether. These are more cheering aspects of the historical evidence, and as worthy of consideration as all the bestiality.

I owe acknowledgements to the scholars who have collected the ancient material concerning gladiators, and particularly to those whose works are mentioned at the end of this book. I am also grateful for permissions to quote from translations of ancient authors. I have introduced a number of amendments into this new edition, and have expanded certain passages.

Gattaiola, 1971 MICHAEL GRANT

1   GLADIATORS IN REPUBLICAN ROME

THE FIRST GLADIATORIAL SHOWS

Herodotus noted that the barbarous Scythians of Thrace performed human sacrifices at funerals, and readers of the *Iliad* are shocked to find the Greek army before Troy celebrating similar rites at the funeral of Patroclus. In Italy, the ceremonies in honour of his death figured prominently on the tomb-paintings of the Etruscans, whose representations of the theme, repeated at one necropolis after another, seem to go back to some famous original version, now lost. These Etruscans, living north of the Tiber in loosely federated city-states which prospered by means of their metal-working and chariots, had a potent, rhythmical art, Hellenizing and orientalizing yet full of native genius. Its best masterpieces were achieved in expressing Etruria's highly ritualized religion.

Yet the networks of chamber-tombs show this to have been a religion of gloom and terror. In particular, the Etruscans seem to have remained faithful to the custom of sacrificing prisoners of war to the shades of their own fallen warriors – the theme of Patroclus' funeral. Sometimes, it is thought, the sacrifices took place in effigy, the living victims being replaced by puppets. Yet there were grisly reversions to the real thing. In the sixth century BC the people of Etruscan Caere (Cerveteri) stoned to death the Greek and Carthaginian prisoners they had captured in a sea-battle off Alalia (Aleria). In 358 BC three hundred and seven Roman prisoners of war were slaughtered as human sacrifices in the forum of Tarquinii. In 40 BC Octavian, the future Augustus, immolated to deceased members of the Julian family three hundred of the principal people of rebel Perusia (Perugia), pointing out with sinister irony that he must allow his Etruscan enemies the rites which belonged to their own national customs. Not long afterwards Virgil, echoing the Homeric rites for Patroclus, made the god-fearing Aeneas perform human sacrifice at the young Prince Pallas' funeral.

Manacled captives there were, consigned to be gifts to the dead –
Victims whose blood would be sprinkled upon the altar flames.

But centuries before the *Aeneid* the custom had started of not just sacrificing prisoners of war but instead setting them to fight to the death against one another in the arena, as gladiators. When the Romans adopted this practice, it was believed at least in some circles (though, as will be seen, it was also possible to take another view) that like many of their other habits, traditions and ceremonies it came to them from Etruria. If so, it presumably came in the days when Rome itself, in the sixth century BC, had been under Etruscan rule. This origin of gladiatorial combats is explicitly described by a Greco-Syrian historian of the Augustan age, Nicolaus of Damascus. Certain surviving features of the Roman games pointed to the same conclusion : for example when a gladiator fell he was hauled out of the arena by a slave dressed as the Etruscan death-demon Charun (whom Virgil made into Charon) and carrying the hammer which was the demon's attribute. Reliefs showing gladiatorial contests appear on grave-urns of the third century BC from Etruria. Moreover, the Latin term for a trainer-manager of gladiators, *lanista*, was believed by some etymologists to be an Etruscan word; and they may well have been right. Incidentally, paintings of the sixth century BC discovered at Tarquinii show that the Etruscans also practised and handed down to Rome another of its characteristic institutions. This was the wild-animal hunt, conducted amid frightful carnage by specialists called *bestiarii*, who did not rank as gladiators and possessed an elaborate organization of their own; in Spain, as earlier in Minoan Crete, their speciality was already bull-fighting. But the combatants on the Etruscan paintings may be criminals thrown to the beasts, anticipating another diabolical Roman custom.

As for the gladiators themselves, an aura of religious sacrifice continued to hang about their combats, particularly in Gaul but also elsewhere. Obviously most spectators just enjoyed the massacre without any such antiquarian reflections. But the more thoughtful ancient writers continued to be well aware that gladiators had originated from these holocausts in honour of the dead. The African Christian Tertullian, writing two centuries after the birth of Christ, described these combats of the amphitheatre as the most famous, the most popular spectacle of all.

What was offered to appease the dead was counted as a funeral rite ... It is called *munus* (a service) from being a service due ... The ancients thought that by this sort of spectacle they rendered a service to the dead, after they had tempered it with a more cultured form of cruelty. For of old, in the belief that the souls of the dead are propitiated with human blood, they used at funerals to sacrifice captives or slaves of poor quality. Afterwards it seemed good to obscure their impiety by making it a pleasure. So after the persons procured had been trained in such arms as they then had and as best they might – their training was to learn to be killed! – they then did them to death on the appointed funeral day at the tombs. So they found comfort for death in murder ...

For such reasons gladiators were sometimes known as *bustuarii* or funeral men. Throughout many centuries of Roman history, these commemorations of the dead were still among the principal occasions for such combats; indeed the cult of deceased and deified emperors provided typical opportunities. Men writing their wills often made provision for gladiatorial duels in connection with their funerals. Early in the first century AD, the people of Pollentia (Pollenzo in Liguria) forcibly prevented the burial of an official, until his heirs had been compelled to provide money for a gladiators' show. Another testator provided for a duel between women chosen for their attractive looks; and another stipulated a contest between boys he had loved, though in this case the public, with unusual chivalry, secured the annulment of the will.

The *munera* – the word is never used for any sort of games other than gladiatorial displays – came to be fixed in December, the time of the Saturnalia. Although the

predecessor of our Christmas, this was also the festival
of the god Saturn, whose name was linked with human
sacrifice. This was because of his identification with the
child-eating Greek god Kronos and, through him, with a
Carthaginian deity who was entitled to the most bloodthirsty offerings. The infernal, agricultural, resurrectional
gods were lovers of human blood. Redemption sacrifices
were especially necessary at a time of transition; and local
munera were in due course extended to birthdays, founda-
tion ceremonies for new buildings, anniversaries of deaths
and of dedications of statues and temples, victories, plagues,
new epochs and centenaries, and so on.

It was mentioned earlier that the institution was sometimes attributed to the Etruscans. Now these, at the height
of their power, had an important dependency in Campania, separated from their main territory by the Tiber and by
Rome and Latium. The Campanians, and the Lucanians
on their southern flank, depicted gladiatorial combats on
their art at an early date. However, it cannot be regarded
as certain that these contests came to them from the
Etruscans, or at least direct from the Etruscans. For Campania, in the fifth century BC, was occupied by the Samnites or Sabellians, hillmen from the interior, who later,
after prolonged struggles, succumbed to Rome (*c.* 290 BC).
Now Samnite paintings show gladiatorial fightings as early
as the first years of the fourth century BC, in advance of
any known representations in Etruria. Down to the first
century BC Romans regarded 'gladiator' and 'Samnite' as
synonymous terms.

In any case, whether it was from Samnium or Etruria
that they came – and perhaps they came from Etruria via

Samnium – these contests took root and flourished in Campania and Lucania, as can be seen in paintings from the Campanian metropolis Capua and from Lucanian Posidonia (Paestum). These pictures show helmeted gladiators carrying shields and lances; they are scarred with wounds and dripping with blood.

Capua long remained a centre of this activity. Capua and another Campanian town, Puteoli, possessed the largest amphitheatres known (until overtaken by the Colosseum), and Campanian fighters continued to have special prestige. Thus as late as AD 249 it was still a subject for boasting at Minturnae that in a four-day show the fatalities included not only ten ferocious bears but eleven leading Campanian gladiators (GLA*diatores* PRI*Mores* CAMP*aniae* XI).

Such, then, were the precedents available to the Romans. For the capital a decisive moment of gladiatorial history was reached in 264 BC, the year when the first Punic War began. At the funeral of Brutus Pera – the man who according to Nicolaus had got the idea from the Etruscans – his two sons for the first time exhibited, in the cattle market, three simultaneous gladiatorial combats. By 216 BC the number of fights given on a single occasion had risen to twenty-two. Ten years later Carthago Nova (Cartagena) in Spain was the scene of similar funeral contests; and the Seleucid monarch Antiochus Epiphanes imported the custom into Syria. Meanwhile at Rome itself this type of entertainment grew until in 174 BC, at Flamininus' games in honour of his father, seventy-four men fought against each other during a display lasting for three days. Then in about 165 the dramatist Terence reported that a performance of his play *The Mother-in-Law* was disrupted by rumours that a gladiatorial show was about to begin. But such contests were already becoming very expensive, and Scipio Aemilianus had to add a contribution when his brother could not afford to give a display on his own account.

In 105 BC, for the first time, the two consuls of the year gave gladiatorial games officially. There was no doubt a religious undercurrent, but the purpose was also to promote toughness and military training and to counteract the soft Greek culture which now was abroad. This xenophobe Roman spirit, which led to such brutalities, was long cherished as a virile idea. One of those who later sang of its glories was Horace:

> Youth must harden its limbs in war,
> Bear harsh poverty like a friend,
> Learn to harry the savage Parthian,
> Riding him down at the spear-point,
> Live life under the sky among
> Urgent perils.

Some of Rome's rulers and thinkers justified gladiatorial games on those grounds.

SPARTACUS AND AFTER

Capua, for centuries the headquarters of gladiators, was also the city which produced the greatest gladiatorial sensation of all time – the outbreak led by Spartacus in 73 BC. What happened was recorded some thirty-five years later by Sallust, in his *Histories*; they are almost entirely lost, but an outline of the events can be recovered from the differing accounts of two Greek writers of the second century AD, Plutarch and Appian.

Spartacus, apparently a man of superior character and intellect, came from Thrace, which was still an independent country though it was already the target of Roman retaliatory raids. He himself had been a Roman soldier, but he deserted and became a brigand. Recaptured by the Romans, he was sold into slavery; and so he became a gladiator in the Capuan school. There he organized a break-out. Seventy of his fellow-gladiators, most of them Gauls or Thracians, accompanied him in the successful attempt. Armed with knives from the kitchens (since gladiators were not allowed weapons of their own), they repulsed their warders and fought their way to freedom. Outside the city walls the band drove back a force of pursuers, from whom it acquired a more professional collection of weapons. With two Gauls, Oenomaus and Crixus, as his fellow-leaders, Spartacus led his force to Mount Vesuvius. There they established themselves in the crater (at that time quiescent and believed to be extinct), and waited for the Romans to besiege them. The Roman commander who arrived was Claudius Glaber, sent by the praetor Publius Varinius to whom the government had entrusted this minor mopping-up operation.

'There was only one way up this hill,' says Plutarch,

and that was a narrow and difficult one, and was closely guarded by Glaber; in every other direction there was nothing but sheer precipitous cliffs. The top of the hill, however, was covered with wild vines and from these the gladiators cut off all the branches that they needed, and then twisted them into strong ladders which were long enough to reach from the top, where they were fastened, right down the cliff face to the plain below. They all got down safely by means of these ladders except for one man who stayed at the top to deal with the arms, and he, once the rest had got down, began to drop the arms down to them, and, when he had finished his task, descended last and reached the plain in safety. The Romans knew nothing of all this, and so the gladiators were able to get round behind them and to throw them into confusion by the unexpectedness of the attack, first routing them and then capturing their camp. And now they were joined by numbers of herdsmen and shepherds of those parts, all sturdy men and fast on their feet. Some of these they armed as regular infantrymen and made use of others as scouts and light troops.

The Romans, whose amateur, political generals often caused them to lose the early battles of a campaign, experienced further humiliating setbacks near Vesuvius and then not far from Herculaneum, and finally the praetor Varinius himself was defeated by the gladiators. They were now free to roam, plunder and ravage throughout Campania and Lucania. Spartacus, then and later, tried to restrain their savagery. But he was not very successful in this, and there were perilous divisions in the high command. For Spartacus himself saw no hope of final victory against the vast reserves of Rome; and so his plan was to move northwards and cross the Alps, thus enabling his men to disperse to their own countries and homes. His colleague Crixus, on the other hand, wanted to go on plundering Italy, and with this aim he left Spartacus, taking the Gaulish and German gladiators with him.

Spartacus did not march to the north straight away, but

spent the winter near Thurii (Terranova di Sibari) in Lucania, planning the next campaign. Meanwhile new recruits poured in – the destitute down-at-heel vagabonds with whom Italy abounded, supplemented by runaway slaves and members of chain-gangs whom the rebels released from the landowners' huge ranches. Horses, too, were collected in considerable numbers, and a cavalry unit was formed.

By the next year the Senate of Rome had at last awoken to the dangers of the situation. Four legions were sent into the field, under the heads of the Roman government themselves, the consuls Lucius Gellius and Lentulus Clodianus. Near Mount Garganus they overwhelmed Crixus' force and killed its leader. Yet Spartacus, on the high ground of Picenum (Marche), managed to encounter each consul separately, and beat both of them in turn. Appian tells how, in mockery of Roman custom, he forced three hundred of his prisoners to fight in gladiatorial combat against one another – to appease the spirit of Crixus.

It was said that at this stage Spartacus considered whether he might not make an attempt upon Rome itself. But, if so, he abandoned the project as unrealistic, and instead persisted in his plan to evacuate the peninsula across the Alps. When he defeated the governor of Cisalpine Gaul (north Italy), the prospects looked promising. Yet something now made him change his mind – perhaps he lost control of his men – and he retreated south again. But now he had to deal with a more distinguished opponent, for the discredited Roman commanders had been superseded by Crassus, a clever millionaire and politician who had also served a valuable military apprenticeship under the great

Sulla. After initial setbacks Crassus succeeded in penning Spartacus into the toe of Italy, across which he then immediately began to construct fortifications in order to block the gladiators' landward exit. Spartacus hoped that Mediterranean pirates, the enemies of Rome, would transport him and his men across the strait to Sicily, but they disappointed him. So instead he broke through the Roman fortifications before they were completed and was back in the open country of the mainland.

Crassus was now increasingly eager to finish Spartacus off quickly and by himself, since Rome, becoming impatient, had appointed his political rival Pompey as his fellow commander. Before Pompey arrived, Crassus seemed to have an opportunity when a further split occurred in the gladiatorial command, from which two more Gaulish officers separated with a force of their own. This was beaten by the Romans, but Spartacus came to its help, and a major battle was fought near the source of the river Silarus (Sele) in Lucania. Crassus inflicted enormous losses upon the gladiators, recapturing the insignia of the defeated consuls and a host of Roman standards. Spartacus again retreated to the southern extremity of Italy. He was victorious in one more battle, but then, against Crassus' huge army, he finally succumbed. Pompey, however, took the credit, because on his way south he was able to engage and destroy some last remnants of Spartacus' followers.

'So,' says Rice Holmes,

perished the heroic gladiator, who had moulded herdsmen, brigands and outcasts into a victorious army, supplied them with weapons and equipment, contrived during two years to feed them and to keep them together, done all that man could do to protect the innocent from their lust and vengeance, nine times defeated Roman armies, and compelled the Roman government to put forth their whole available power in order to subdue him.

The previous decades had seen slave-wars which had torn a gaping hole in the society of the ancient world, but this one, led by gladiators, was the most terrible of them all – and ten Roman legions were needed to put it down. Spartacus' name lived on, and he became the hero of Marxism. His story has now been told in a moving novel by Arthur Koestler. After the downfall of the gladiatorial army there came that merciless vengeance which always awaited recalcitrant slaves. Six thousand prisoners were crucified along the Appian Way, from Rome all the way to Capua, where the outbreak had begun.

Appalled by the menace it had only averted after so much shock and effort, the Roman government clamped an iron discipline upon future generations of gladiators. Yet they continued to cause political anxiety. For Roman strong-arm politicians and war-lords now showed increasing signs of tampering with the gladiator in their own personal in-terests, envisaging him as a useful auxiliary to the private armies with which they exerted pressure on the state. At the time of Catiline's crackpot right-wing conspiracy (63 BC) the danger from gladiators seemed especially great at Rome, and Sallust reports the senate's decision that the troops of fighters stationed in the capital should be sent away and split up among Capua and other towns. But at Capua, too, Catiline's fellow-conspirators tried to make friends with the inmates of the gladiators' school, and one of his eminent supporters practised duelling with them to curry favour. However, before any harm could come of this, the conspiracy came to a violent end.

Later, at the beginning of the Civil War (49 BC), Pompey's supporters were worried in case Caesar might call up his gladiators at Capua to serve in his army. The Pompeian consul Lentulus had an idea of getting in first, but according to one of Cicero's letters Pompey instead 'very cleverly distributed the gladiators two apiece to heads of families. There were 5,000 heavy armed gladiators in the school. They were said to meditate a sortie. Pompey's was a wise provision for the safety of the state.' That is to say, the gladiators were both disarmed as a potential military unit and employed as bodyguards. But then again, in the subsequent series of civil wars after Caesar's death, Antony had gladiators at Cyzicus (in north-western Asia Minor) who were ready to fight for him against Octavian (Augustus), remaining loyal even after the decisive battle of Actium was lost.

Meanwhile it had become customary for gladiatorial displays to be put on not only by victorious generals, as a feature of their Triumphs, but also by officials of every rank. The functionaries known as aediles, for example, sought to attract popularity by giving *ludi honorarii*, supplementary games attached to theatre and circus performances. It was one of these aediles, writes Suetonius, that Julius Caesar, in memory of his father (65 BC),

put on a gladiatorial show, but had collected so immense a troop of combatants that his terrified political opponents rushed a bill through the House, limiting the number that anyone might keep in Rome; consequently far fewer pairs fought than had been advertised.

Nevertheless the diminished troop still amounted to 320 pairs! Two years later, during the time of the anxiety about Catiline which was mentioned earlier, the senate passed a measure disqualifying from office any candidate who had financed such a show during the two years immediately preceding his election;[1] and Cicero was furious with a political enemy, Vatinius, because he sought popularity by flouting this decision while the election was actually under way.

Caesar's fourfold Triumph over his enemies (46 BC) was the occasion for a display of unprecedented splendour and slaughter. In addition to appallingly lavish wild-beast hunts, a gladiatorial battle was staged in the Circus with five hundred infantry, thirty cavalry and twenty elephants on either side. Caesar was also the first to stage such contests in memory of a woman – his daughter Julia.

Gladiators' fights were not only popular; they were also lucrative for their promoters. 'Really,' writes Cicero to his rich friend Atticus, 'what a fine troop you have bought! I hear your gladiators are fighting splendidly. If you had cared to let them out, you would have cleared your expenses on the two shows you gave.'

1. Exceptions were made for dates explicitly fixed by wills.

2 THE GLADIATORS'
PROFESSION

WHO WERE THE GLADIATORS?

Gladiators of all epochs – or at any rate people who, trained or untrained, had to fight in the arena – included countless thousands of prisoners of war. The Hebrew renegade historian Josephus describes how Titus dealt with his captives from the Jewish rebellion. 'The number of those destroyed in contests with wild beasts or with one another or in the flames exceeded 2,500. Yet to the Romans, notwithstanding the myriad forms in which their victims perished, all this seemed too light a penalty.'

Those compelled to fight gladiatorial duels included not only prisoners of war but condemned criminals. Among them were numerous Christians, at times when persecution fell heavily on their faith; and many won imperishable fame as martyrs. For fighting in the arena was one of the sentences earned by the sacrilege imputed against members of the Christian religion because of their apparently anarchistic, anti-social, treasonable refusal to sacrifice to the emperor. The martyrologies often tell of Christians who were forced, as gladiatorial novices were forced, to run the gauntlet. At other times they were thrown to the wild beasts. One such persecution was organized in Gaul by an official of Marcus Aurelius, who although of exemplary high-mindedness deplored the Christian martyrs as hysterical exhibitionists.

His regional representative allowed Christians who had succumbed to a wave of popular violence to be made into human sacrificial victims (*trinqui*), in accordance with an archaic Gaulish ritual. This was the sequel to a complaint by the chief priest of the Gallic provinces that, owing to the current high cost of gladiators, the entertainment he was obliged to give would reduce him to destitution. Pending price-legislation, Aurelius had authorized his agent to provide the man with *trinqui* at six gold pieces a head.

These were criminals condemned to death. The crimes which led to the arena were murder, treason, robbery and arson.

We can turn to Josephus again for a holocaust of such malefactors, conducted by the puppet monarch Agrippa at Berytus (Beirut). Into his costly new amphitheatre, although such shows had been foreign to Hebrew custom until Herod had introduced them, Agrippa 'sent in 700 men to fight another 700. All these men were malefactors set aside for this purpose . . . in this way he brought about the utter annihilation of these men.' Criminals sentenced to forced labour were often obliged to serve as gladiators, and were sentenced to three years of combat and two years in the schools. This sort of conviction was comparable to being condemned to the mines, except that the former sentence, although affording only a relatively slender chance of survival, was regarded as less severe. Sometimes penalties were differentiated according to social class: thus for certain crimes which in the case of a slave would involve execution, free men or freedmen (ex-slaves) were condemned to fight in the arena instead. This did not, of course, make them gladiators, unless they were trained first, as those required to provide this sort of sport not always were – and indeed as gladiators became more expensive in the second century AD the use of untrained criminals in the amphitheatre increased.

Correspondence between the emperor Trajan and Pliny the younger, who was his governor of Bithynia-Pontus (northern Asia Minor), includes reference to a disciplinary problem arising when towns of the region allowed such convicts to leave the gladiatorial service or the mines in order to perform the duties of public slaves or minor civil servants. Pliny consults the emperor because he cannot decide what to do with such cases.

On the one hand, to send them back again after a long interval to their respective punishments (many of them being now grown old, and behaving, as I am assured, with sobriety and modesty) would, I thought, be proceeding against them too severely; on the other, to retain convicts in the public service seemed not altogether decent. I considered, at the same time, that to support these people in idleness would be a useless expense to the public; and to leave them to starve would be dangerous.

The imperial voice of Rome which replied was, as usual, chilling, harsh-sounding, yet (given the state of contemporary society and thought) not unjust.

We are to remember that you were sent into Bithynia for the particular purpose of correcting those many abuses with which it appeared to be overrun. Now none stands more in need of reformation than that convicts should not only be set at liberty (as your letter informs me) without authority, but actually restored to the station of respectable officials. Those therefore among them who have been convicted within these ten years, and whose sentence has not been reversed by proper authority, must be sent back again to their respective punishments. But where more than ten years have elapsed since their conviction, and they are grown old and infirm, let them be distributed in such employments as approach penal servitude : that is, either to attend upon the public baths, cleanse the common sewers, or repair the streets and highways, the usual offices to which such persons are assigned.

Most gladiators, at Rome and elsewhere, were slaves; but in addition there were always some free men who became gladiators because they wanted to. The profession was a refuge for social outcasts. The poet Manilius early in the first century AD, and Tertullian two centuries later, bear witness that desperate and violent men would take to this career; and so did adventurers made restless by the monotony of the *pax Romana*. And then again when the emperor Septimius Severus decided that his praetorian guard, which was now predominantly German, should exclude Italians altogether, some of the dismissed guardsmen – those who did not go underground and take to brigandage – joined the gladiatorial schools. Moreover, as we learn from numerous inscriptions, it was quite customary for retired gladiators to return to the profession. They must have been in considerable demand, since Tiberius had to pay 1,000 gold pieces in order to persuade such veterans to make a single appearance.

These ex-fighters, if they had been slaves during their period of service, were liberated on retirement, and when they rejoined it was as free volunteers that they did so. New recruits, too, regularly included a proportion of free men. These were generally derived from the lowest-ranking category of free persons, namely the freedmen who had themselves been slaves or were the sons of slaves. In inscriptions recording lists of gladiators, the free are normally distinguishable from the slaves by the form of their names. Thus an inscription from the island of Thasos shows two free men to ten slaves, while at Aegae (Nemrut Kalesi) in western Asia Minor the figures are five and three respectively. Free fighters were more sought after than slaves, presumably because they showed greater enthusiasm. As Petronius makes Trimalchio's dinner-guest Echion the rag-merchant remark, 'We're going to have a holiday with a three days' show that's the best ever – and not just a hack troupe of gladiators but freedmen for the most part.'

An exceptional feat of survival was claimed by the gladiator Publius Ostorius at Pompeii – a freedman and voluntary fighter, combatant in no less than fifty-one fights. Such a volunteer was offered a bonus if he survived the term of his contract. And yet, for its duration, he had to swear the terrible oath of submission to be burnt with fire, shackled with chains, whipped with rods, and killed with steel (*uri, uinciri, uerberari, ferroque necari*). He must also declare his subjection officially to a functionary of state, the praetor, and indeed the whole proceedings compelled recognition of his new master's right of life and death. For the period of his engagement, he had become no more than a slave. Nevertheless he could still buy back his freedom, even before he had fought; and the rhetorical schools, which gave the empire its university training, made play with this sort of situation. For example the educationalist Quintilian, in the later first century AD, quotes a theme for a declamation in which the sister defends herself against the brother whom she had often redeemed from the gladiatorial school, when he brought an action against her demanding the infliction of a similar mutilation because she had cut off his thumb while he slept: 'You deserved,' she cries, 'to have all your fingers,' meaning thereby, 'You deserved to be a gladiator all your days.' Another romantic theme is pursued by the second-century philosopher Lucian of Samosata, a Greco-Syrian who hated the arena. His essay *Toxaris* tells how, at Amastris (Amasra) on the Black Sea coast, Sisinnes enrolled to fight a gladiator for a fixed sum of 10,000 drachmae in order to help his friend out of a difficulty. Another such story told of the alleged enrolment of a young aristocrat as a gladiator in order to pay for his father's funeral.

Noblemen, or even Roman citizens, who took to such a career were a great source of excitement and reprobation for moralists and satirists. The volunteers from this high social class were relatively few, but conspicuous. A notorious Spaniard, Lucius Cornelius Balbus of Gades (Cadiz), twice tried to force a political enemy to fight as a gladiator, and on his refusal had him burnt alive. At one of Caesar's shows a patrician entered the arena with a barrister who had been a member of the senate, and they fought to the death. Cicero repeatedly sneered at Antony's brother Lucius for fighting as a gladiator in Asia Minor, and cutting his opponent's throat. Similar contests involving members of respected families are recorded under the first two emperors; and it pleased Caligula to compel many knights and senators to fight. But this was regarded as a scandal, and Tacitus records one of the few disciplinary measures taken by the transient ruler Vitellius (AD 69).

Strict orders were issued that Romans (knights) were not to disgrace themselves by performing in the games and the arena. Previous emperors had driven them to this sort of thing by offering payment or, more often, by the use of force. Moreover, a number of Italian towns vied with one another in holding out financial inducements to undesirables among the younger generation.

Writing at about the same period as Tacitus, the satirical poet Juvenal lashes himself into a fury at the situation, real or imaginary, in which a possessor of the glorious name of Sempronius Gracchus demeaned himself by following the gladiatorial career.

> Still, when the emperor turns to playing a fiddle, no wonder
> Nobles act on the stage. Below this level there's nothing.
> Ah, but there is! The games! Go there for the ultimate
>   scandal,
> Looking at Gracchus . . .

That is to say the offence of being a gladiator, for a member of the upper classes, is comparable to acting – though even worse. Indeed, it is a logical step downwards from the one to the other, and emperors had sometimes forced such men to fight in the arena just because they had already disgraced themselves by appearing on the stage. A discredited senator assured Marcus Aurelius, no doubt amid widespread embarrassment, that he saw around him many praetors who had been his fellow-fighters in the amphitheatre.

Another rich source of scandal was the adoption of the gladiatorial career by women. The mind reels at the thought of what a female Roman gladiator must have been like; but they did exist. Domitian, who had a lethal sense of humour, enjoyed their shows, some of which he organized by torch-light. A relief in the British Museum, from Halicarnassus (Bodrum) in the eastern Aegean, shows two women gladiators fighting; inscriptions from the same area record female combatants named Achillia and Amazon – and it is to Amazons, of course, that the poets compared them. Petronius mentions a female *essedaria*, a gladiatress fighting from a British-style chariot. What was, however, regarded as especially disgraceful was the participation of noblewomen in such activities. According to Tacitus, this practice increased to an alarming degree of frequency in the ninth year of Nero, AD 63. Moreover, the same reign introduced a note of novelty; for when the Armenian monarch Tiridates visited Italy, the emperor's freedman Patrobius organized at Puteoli (Pozzuoli) a special sort of show in which there were female as well as male fighters, of every age – and all of them were Africans.

Juvenal brought the full force of his scathing ridicule to bear on women gladiators.

> Who has not seen the dummies of wood they slash at and batter
> Whether with swords or with spears, going through all the manoeuvres?

These are the girls who blast on the trumpets in honour of
    Flora.
Or, it may be, they have deeper designs, and are really prepar-
    ing
For the arena itself. How can a woman be decent
Sticking her head in a helmet, denying the sex she was born
    with?
Manly feats they adore, but they wouldn't want to be men,
Poor weak things (they think), how little they really enjoy it!
What a great honour it is for a husband to see, at an auction
Where his wife's effects are up for sale, belts, shin-guards,
Arm-protectors and plumes!
Hear her grunt and groan as she works at it, parrying,
    thrusting;
See her neck bent down under the weight of her helmet.
Look at the rolls of bandage and tape, so her legs look like
    tree trunks,
Then have a laugh for yourself, after the practice is over,
Armour and weapons put down, and she squats as she uses
    the vessel.
Ah, degenerate girls from the line of our praetors and consuls,
Tell us, whom have you seen got up in any such fashion,
Panting and sweating like this? No gladiator's wench,
No tough strip-tease broad would ever so much as attempt it.

In AD 200, after a particularly vigorous outburst of
gladiatorial contests between women, the emperor Septimius Severus, whose régime for all its harsher side was largely
in the hands of enlightened lawyers, forbade female combatants altogether.

IMPERIAL SHOWS AND SCHOOLS

There seemed no end to public entertainments of one sort or another at Rome. First there were the regular functions. The number of days in each year given up to annual games and spectacles of one sort or another in the city was startlingly large, and increased continually. Already 66 in the time of Augustus, it had risen to 135 under Marcus Aurelius, and to 175 or more in the fourth century. Yet these are figures which take no account of the enormous and repeated special shows given by each successive emperor.

These shows included a profuse outlay of gladiators. Augustus offered 'extraordinary' gladiatorial games – that is to say displays over and above the regular shows given by officials – three times in his own name and five times in the names of his sons and grandsons. By this enormous expense and carnage, involving no less than 10,000 fighters, he almost monopolized such entertainments, so that the prestige which they earned should be his alone. Another very ambitious project was organized by Claudius, whose Triumph of AD 44 staged in the Campus Martius enacted the realistic capture and sack of a town, followed by the surrender of the enemy's leaders. During the shortlived supremacy of Vitellius, his generals Caecina and Valens gave massive gladiatorial shows at Cremona and Bononia (Bologna) respectively, and later, on an unprecedented scale, celebrated the emperor's birthday by combats in all the two hundred and sixty-five districts of Rome. At the dedication of the Colosseum, Titus gave a hundred-day festival attended by 'every nation of the world'.

Then in AD 107 Trajan celebrated his victories in Dacia

(Rumania) by a four months' period of entertainments during which he sent not only 10,000 animals but also 10,000 gladiators into the amphitheatre – a figure equal to the total of Augustus' lavishness during his whole reign. Nor was this by any means the whole of Trajan's effort. A fragment of a calendar, discovered not very long ago at Ostia, gives a few statistics regarding further gladiatorial contests which he subsequently gave during the years 108–113. The inscription records two comparatively minor displays, involving 350 and 202 combatants respectively, and a record event lasting 117 days in which 4,941 pairs were engaged. Altogether between 106 and 114 the number of gladiators fighting under imperial auspices reached a horrifying total of at least 23,000.

Later emperors did their best not to disappoint. Thousands of fighters were matched against one another at Philip the Arabian's celebration of the millenary of Rome (AD 248), and then again repeatedly – trained or untrained – in the Triumphs of subsequent decades which exhibited thousands of war prisoners, symbolizing the empire's re-emergence from anarchic disruption into the formidable totalitarian machine of late antiquity.

The arch-patron of this gigantic activity was always the emperor. Gladiatorial entertainments had become a wholly indispensable feature of the services a ruler had to provide, in order to keep his popularity and his job. Emperors themselves had to attend the shows – and watch their step. They were closely observed by thousands; all eyes scrutinized their demeanour to see whether it was generous or grudging, matey or stand-offish, attentive or negligent, sadistic or relatively humane. What these crowds saw and heard of their Caesars in the arena was recorded in innumerable anecdotes. Some of the impressions created by emperors in the amphitheatre were grotesque. Even their conversations were overheard, and it was noted, for example, that Domitian, 'throughout every gladiatorial show would chat, sometimes in very serious tones, with a little boy who had a grotesquely small head and always stood at his knee dressed in red. Once he was heard to ask the child: "Can you guess why I have just appointed Mettius Rufus Prefect of Egypt?" '

Emperors watching the gladiatorial shows were conspicuous, vulnerable, and liable to public pressures which could not be displayed elsewhere. That was one of the reasons why the games were not popular with a few rulers such as Marcus Aurelius. He directed that if a gladiator was freed as a result of popular outcry in the amphitheatre the liberation was to be annulled; Aurelius found the sport boring, and indeed he was unenthusiastic about Roman public entertainments in general. Earlier, Tiberius had incurred unfriendly speculation since he, too, was one of the small number of emperors who did not enjoy these combats, and showed it. 'A gladiatorial display,' says Tacitus,

was given in the names of the emperor's adopted son Germanicus and his own son Drusus. The latter was abnormally fond of bloodshed. Admittedly it was worthless blood, but the public was shocked and his father Tiberius was reported to have reprimanded him. The emperor himself kept away. Various reasons were given – his dislike of crowds, or his natural glumness, or unwillingness to be compared with Augustus, who had cheerfully attended. It was also suggested, though I would scarcely believe it, that he deliberately gave his son a chance to show his forbidding character – and win unpopularity.

Tacitus does not suggest that Tiberius may have found these contests either tedious or inhumane, though the former is a likely enough explanation of his aloofness and even the latter, for a man so deeply imbued with Greek philosophy as Tiberius, is not impossible.

Here was a vast and popular imperial activity. Yet was there also a note of shame somewhere? The student of numismatics might feel inclined to suggest that there is. Lacking modern means of publicity, the rulers of Rome were accustomed to blazon forth to the world on their varied, ubiquitous coinage the themes of self-praise which they felt did themselves the most credit. Certain topics, such as military victory and loyalty, become monotonously repetitive; but there were also noteworthy omissions. For example, the huge presentations of money to the soldiery, which helped to ruin the empire, are passed over in silence. Yet it was considered respectable and indeed praiseworthy to mention distributions, in cash and kind, to the *civilian* population. In regard to public entertainments – the other half of *panem et circenses* – there is again an adjustment of emphasis. Some of these amusements find their place on the coinage; but not others. Thus animal hunts and combats (the fights conducted by *bestiarii*) are explicitly recorded on the coins, which depict, for example, wild beasts massacred at games given by Antoninus Pius and Philip. Indeed the former, though one of the most enlightened of Roman rulers, labels a slaughtered elephant MVNIFICENTIA AVG (*usti*) – 'the generosity of the emperor'. Yet the gladiator-fighting, which accompanied these massacres of wild beasts, is one of the themes that the vast, comprehensive range of imperial Roman coin-types wholly fails to include.[1] It is true that Titus and Domitian show a picture of the Colosseum on very rare coins, and Severus Alexander and Gordian III repeat the type on medallions. But the permanent absence of gladiators themselves from coins and medallions contrasts strongly with the willingness to depict victims of animal-fights – and cannot be anything but deliberate. It can only be surmised that the officials, whoever they were, who chose these designs left some standing instruction at the mint about this: presumably on the grounds that the spilling of human blood in sport, although regarded as a necessity in order to keep the population sweet, was not actually something to boast about.

The Caesars very soon had to appoint a high official to look after this whole activity on their behalf. Caligula, for example, employed such a man. But it proved to be an unenviable post, if, as was reported, the emperor 'watched the manager of his gladiatorial and wild-beast shows being flogged with chains for several days running, and had him killed only when the smell of suppurating brains became insupportable'. Nevertheless under the next ruler, Claudius, the office was regularized, its holder being known as the *procurator a muneribus* or *munerum*. He and his chief derived the human resources for their shows from the imperial gladiators' schools. Under the Republic the oldest known schools were at Capua in Campania – operating

1. For gladiators on a single local coinage of Asia Minor, see below, p. 52.

under conditions which produced the break-out of Spartacus. Before the end of the Republic there was a similar establishment at Rome, perhaps near the Theatre of Pompey. Then Horace mentions a gladiatorial Ludus Aemilius; and there was another Augustan school (unless they were the same) beside the new Amphitheatre of Statilius Taurus. This school was privately owned, no doubt by the Statilian family which was devoted to the arena.

But from now on the leading gladiatorial training centres were imperially owned. Three important imperial schools (in addition to the one specializing in animal shows) were concentrated at Rome, and the largest of them, under a high-ranking official, was the Great School (Ludus Magnus) in the region of the Via Labicana and Via S. Giovanni in Laterano, perhaps founded by Claudius; its excavation started in 1960. An ancient town-plan (the *Forma Urbis Romae*) indicates that this institution possessed its own elliptical arena, with much less seating than an amphitheatre, and a larger fighting space in proportion. The lodging accommodation seems to have been divided into sections or Halls, according to the status of gladiators.

In other parts of Italy there were imperial schools at Capua and Ravenna;[2] it is not certain whether their counterpart at Praeneste (Palestrina) was taken over by the emperors or not. At Pompeii, although it has been asserted that the town had no resident gladiators, there was probably another such school, since inscriptions referring to members of the profession as 'Julianus', 'Augustianus' and 'Neronianus' seem to allude to imperial troops of gladiators in the town. The excavated building which has been

2. Julius Caesar had made plans for the latter.

identified as a gladiators' barracks since it contains paintings, *graffiti* and inscriptions relating to their activities was presumably a training school as well. Nearly a hundred rooms were grouped round a rectangular space of some 53 by 42 metres. Some of them were on an upper floor, reached by a staircase leading up to a wooden gallery, of which part has now been reconstructed. The cells on the two floors are between three and four metres square, without windows; these were the grim, dark and dank quarters in which gladiators had to live. On their premises at Pompeii were found sixty-three skeletons, of people who lost their lives in the eruption of Vesuvius (AD 79).

Outside Italy, there was an imperial gladiators' school at Alexandria; a papyrus of AD 260 tells of clothing requisitioned on its behalf. Very probably, also, there were other schools in many provinces of the empire – perhaps in nearly all of them. At least in the case of the smaller of these institutions, several such schools are likely to have been united under the administration of a single official.

Under the general control of these directors, each school possessed a large and complex staff. Many inscriptions commemorate the professional instructors (*doctores*). The teaching of gladiators was a highly elaborate affair involving expertise appreciated by those members of the public who attended the games for something more than blood and thrills. There was an elaborate corpus of gladiatorial theory, adjusted to the various branches of the profession. 'Each branch', concluded Ludwig Friedländer,

had its special instructor. Novices practised with wooden swords at a man of straw or a post (the two-metre high *palus*).

The weapons used in more adept practice were heavier than those used in the arena; possibly the very weighty ones found at Pompeii were for practice. The fencing of the gladiators was a science, and its technical expressions generally understood. Quintilian compares the speeches of counsel with the fencing of gladiators; 'the second stroke becomes the third, if the first be made to make the opponent thrust; or becomes the fourth, if there be a double feint, so that there are two bouts of parrying and riposte'.

No doubt most of the spectators could not follow all this technical stuff, though some of them obviously did.

Training standards were extremely high. Pliny the elder criticized the inmates of Caligula's school for the exacting reason that very few of them could refrain from blinking when a weapon was brandished in their faces. Yet in spite of the expert instruction available Julius Caesar, in his desire to give his gladiators the best tuition available, had gone outside the schools to mobilize expert amateur instructors. 'His new gladiators,' says Suetonius, 'were trained in private houses by Roman knights and even senators who happened to be masters-at-arms. Letters of his survive, begging these trainers to give their pupils individual instruction in the art of fighting.'

Discipline was severe, with ruthless punishments. The prison in the gladiators' barracks at Pompeii was so low that its inmates could only sit or lie. Within its walls in addition to some of the skeletons mentioned above, were found leg-irons for ten prisoners. No arms were allowed in the schools, for fear of outbreaks – or suicides. Symmachus in the fourth century AD rather unsympathetically tells a harrowing story of twenty-nine Saxon prisoners of war, who despite supervision succeeded in doing away with each other *en masse*, rather than fight in the arena.

On the other hand scrupulous attention was invested in the gladiators' health. Their schools were judiciously situated in favourable climates, and equipped with first-class doctors. Indeed, in the second century AD one of the most famous medical men of all time, Galen of Pergamum (Bergama), served as a gladiators' doctor in his native Asia Minor, at the age of twenty-nine, before rising to the position of Marcus Aurelius' personal physician. When he was working with these fighters, Galen claimed that his attention to their health and horrible wounds was responsible for a substantial reduction of mortality. The schools were also provided with resident medical consultants to check the men's diet, and both Galen and a leading doctor of the preceding century, Scribonius Largus, concern themselves with this aspect. Gladiators were called *hordearii*, barley men, because of the amount of barley that they ate, a muscle-building food but (combined with beans as it was at Pergamum) criticized by Galen for making the flesh soft. Cicero's encyclopaedic contemporary Varro reported that effective results were obtained by swallowing ashes, of a special kind, after exercises. Inscriptions also record the services of skilled masseurs (*unctores*). Other staff of the schools included accountants, armourers, morticians, and security guards.

The emperors' staffs were active in the commercial traffic of buying and selling gladiators, and Caligula, who personally conducted auctions of properties fallen vacant through executions or other causes, made very profitable sales. Some of the people obliged to attend these auctions

were forced by the irresistible pressures of imperial sales-
manship into bankruptcy or suicide. A less catastrophic
but still inconvenient shock awaited Aponius Saturninus,
who on one such occasion fell asleep. Caligula 'warned the
auctioneer to keep an eye on the senator who kept nodding
his head. Before the bidding ended, Aponius had unwit-
tingly bought thirteen gladiators for a total of 90,000 gold
pieces.'

Some of the Caesars also kept up an ancient Campanian
(and perhaps Etruscan) custom of staging gladiatorial
shows to entertain their guests at private dinner-parties.
Domitian gave parties of this kind at Albanum, and the
practice was maintained or revived by two other rulers
of unedifying tastes, Lucius Verus and Elagabalus. For such
purposes the emperors kept their own private domestic
troop of gladiators, supervised by ex-slaves.

ORGANIZATION THROUGHOUT THE EMPIRE

The pre-eminence of the emperor as a giver of gladiators'
displays left some room for others, but their powers in the
matter were jealously controlled. In 22 BC Augustus ruled
that no official should organize such contests except the
praetors (the highest traditional functionaries below the
consuls), and even they were only to act on the basis of a
special senatorial decree each time. Augustus also laid it
down that the praetors should hold games only twice a
year, and with never more than 120 combatants. Fifteen
years later he added a further restriction by cutting off the
praetors' shows from state aid. Even so Claudius evidently

felt that these officials were too senior to be safely entrusted with the privilege of providing gladiatorial entertainments, because he transferred the right, or rather duty,
to the more junior, uninfluential and numerous quaestors,
with whom it generally remained.[3] Just occasionally however a very wealthy man, if thoroughly trusted by the
emperor, was still allowed to give games while holding
offices other than the quaestorship. For example at the
end of the second century AD the future emperor Gordian
I, as aedile, not only broke records with a loathsome slaughter of wild animals (including 300 Mauretanian ostriches,
200 deer and 200 chamois) but gave during his single year
of office no less than twelve gladiatorial displays, one a
month, each with at least 150 pairs of gladiators and some
with 500.

But quite early on in the imperial epoch, perhaps under
Domitian, private citizens had been forbidden to keep
gladiators of their own at Rome. Elsewhere however there
was no such veto. In other parts of Italy (as in the provinces) gladiatorial displays were constantly arranged by
private individuals, and there are hosts of inscriptions
testifying to the private initiatives that made them possible.
The holder (*editor*) of such shows had his moment of local
glory. While they were proceeding, he had the right to
wear the insignia of a high official. He earned the rewards
of patronage by presenting many seats free of charge, and
hired out others for profit, or as a contribution to some

3. Nero made this optional, Domitian compulsory again (on ten
days in December). He sometimes lent the quaestors gladiators of
his own. From the time of Severus Alexander those quaestors who
were not imperial nominees received subventions.

popular public work. The poet Martial, in praise of the successful gladiator Hermes, describes him as 'a source of wealth to ticket-sellers' (*divitiae locariorum*).

The annually elected chief officials of towns, their duumvirs (*duoviri*) and aediles, staged gladiatorial combats, with especially grand ones expected from the *quinquennales* elected every five years, who were entrusted with special religious duties. Also prominent among those who sponsored games were the city-priests of a community – which would seem a strange feature of such brutalities, were it not for their religious origin. But, outside Rome, there were many other givers of games too, and Martial is extremely caustic and snobbish about the low social status of some of the men who succeeded in achieving this ambition. He complains that a shoe-maker sponsored contests at the cultured city of Bononia, and a fuller at Mutina (Modena), wondering sarcastically which will be the first town to have a show organized by a publican. Sometimes men went into partnership in order to present gladiatorial fights; inscriptions refer to such associates (*socii*), or speak of the management in the plural.

The satirist Persius sees himself giving a gladiatorial display, with free distributions attached, in honour of an alleged German victory by Caligula.

> Haven't you heard, friend? a laurelled
> Dispatch has arrived from Caesar, announcing
> Victory, the pick of the Germans routed ... I'm putting on a
>   little show
> Myself, to celebrate the occasion and the gods
> And the Emperor's guiding spirit – with a hundred pairs
> Of gladiators ...

Oh, and I'm having a largesse of bread,
And meat, and oil distributed to the populace.

Petronius' rag-merchant gossips about the holders of such shows, and the use they made of them to win popularity for electoral purposes.

My old friend Titus has a big heart and a hot head. Maybe this, maybe that, but something at all events. I'm a close friend of his and he does nothing by halves. He'll give us cold steel, no quarter and the slaughterhouse right in the middle where all the stands can see it. And he's got the wherewithal – he was left thirty million when his poor father died. Even if he spent four hundred thousand, his pocket won't feel it and he'll go down in history. He's got some big brutes already, and a woman who fights in a chariot ... But I can almost smell the dinner Mammaea is going to give us – two denarii apiece for me and the family. If he really does it, he'll make off with all Norbanus' votes, I tell you he'll win at a canter ...

The giver of a show might purchase his gladiators, or might collect them himself; they could be hired for a single hour. In a very few places, including probably Praeneste (Palestrina), they could be drawn from a local training centre. But the sponsor was more likely to commission a trainer-manager to recruit and look after most or all of his team. These shady, reviled figures bear the name of *lanista*, which was probably Etruscan in origin, and called to mind (perhaps with etymological accuracy) the word *lanius*, a butcher. *Lanistae* were everywhere during the Republic and early empire, and thereafter they were still much to be seen except in the capital itself. At this period, remarks Jérôme Carcopino, the organization of these bloody games left no room for improvement. In the Italian *municipia* and in the provincial towns, the local magistrates whose duty it was annually to provide the *munera* called in the advice of specialist contractors, the *lanistae*. These contractors, whose trade shares in Roman law and literature the same infamy that attaches to that of the pander or procurer, were in sober fact Death's middlemen. The *lanista* would hire out his troops of gladiators, at the best figure he could comand, to duumvir or aedile for combats in which about half were bound to lose their lives.

Maintaining a troop (*familia*) at his own expense, buying and selling and letting gladiators, organizing games for profit, he was *infamis*, reviled and beyond the pale; the poet Martial couples the trade with libellous informers and liars.

Owing to the unpleasant associations of the word *lanista*, we find one of them euphemistically describing himself as 'the business manager of a gladiatorial troop' (*negotiator familiae gladiatoriae*). Another, Gaius Salvius Capito, reveals the smallness of the capital on which such men could work, and speculate, since out of nineteen fighters in his troop only one was his own, the rest having been entrusted to him by ten other masters. A man who advertised a show on the walls of Pompeii, Numerius Festus Ampliatus, seems to have been an itinerant *lanista*. The existence of commercial travellers in this field is illustrated by Suetonius' story of the emperor Vitellius' unstable relations with his friend Asiaticus.

Vitellius based many important political decisions on what the lowest performers in the theatre or arena told him, and relied particularly on the advice of his freedman Asiaticus. Asiati-

cus had been Vitellius' slave and catamite, but soon grew tired
of this role and ran away. After a while he was discovered
selling cheap drinks at Puteoli, and put in chains until Vitellius
ordered his release and made him his favourite. However, Asiaticus behaved so insolently, and so thievishly as well, that Vitellius sold him to an itinerant trainer of gladiators; but impulsively
bought him back when he was just about to take part in the
final match of a gladiatorial contest . . .

The emperor, like any other slave-owner, was allowed
by law to sell his slaves into the arena, and this right was
not limited until the slightly humaner times of the second
century AD, when Hadrian insisted that slaves could not
be sent to the gladiatorial schools at least until their master
had made an explanatory declaration to a magistrate. The
great jurists of the age concerned themselves with such
problems; and as tastes continued to become a little more
fastidious, Macrinus (AD 217–18) was criticized for senten-
cing runaway slaves to the arena.

As to the western provinces of the empire, Scipio Africanus
had given gladiatorial games at Carthago Nova (Cartagena)
as early as 206 BC. From Spain again we have a valuable
document of 44 BC, the 'Lex Ursonensis' from Urso (Osuna),
indicating that town officials, duumvirs and aediles, were
obliged to give 'games or dramatic shows' every year. The
minimum rates of expenditure were fixed, but the sponsors
could receive grants in aid, and local corporations might
supplement available funds by private bequests or gifts,
for example those contributed by individuals out of gratitude for their election to municipal offices. As in Italy,
priests figured prominently among the holders of gladia-

torial contests; this seems to have been an optional activity for city-priests but obligatory for the more senior priests of whole provinces.

Some sponsors of these entertainments in the provinces record on inscriptions that they organized their displays at the wish, or demand, of the people (*ex voluntate populi, postulante populo*). But other epigraphic evidence indicates that there were also imperial interventions and subsidies, when the games took place 'through the indulgence of the emperor' – the same phrase as a city (Patrae) used when it was permitted to issue its own coins. Like all financial burdens upon the ruling classes of the provinces, this obligation, or virtual obligation, to give gladiatorial shows tended to become intolerably heavy. However, an official or priest charged to furnish such a display could appeal against the requirement. Indeed, Marcus Aurelius' senate sympathetically lessened the financial commitment. The decree, together with a speech by an unknown senator, appears on an inscription found at Italica (Seville) (the 'Lex Italicensis'). It fixes maximum sale prices for the various categories of gladiators throughout the empire. Aurelius' conscription of gladiators into the armed forces had raised their market-value to a prohibitive level. One effect, mentioned earlier, was a *cri de coeur* by the chief priest of the Gauls. That was temporarily met by a cheap supply of condemned criminals, but now came this general fixing of prices. It was a gesture towards the wealthy classes, whose support the emperor needed in a time of military crisis. Simultaneously Aurelius helped the *lanistae* by lightening their taxation. The exchequer was the loser, but 'imperial money should be pure'!

Evidence for the west can be matched from the Greek-speaking provinces of the Roman commonwealth. These eastern regions were far less squeamish and sparing about gladiatorial shows than was supposed a few years ago. When the Seleucid monarch Antiochus Epiphanes introduced them into Syria in the second century BC there was at first some local resistance. But from early imperial times we have ample proof that the sport flourished throughout the Mediterranean area. There is even one town-coinage, at Synnada (Suhut) in central Asia Minor under Gallienus (253–68), which depicts a gladiatorial combat[4] – a dubious distinction not found in the west.

In the oriental provinces, as in the west, some of the holders of games were private persons. Inscriptional evidence from Thasos records gladiators belonging to a woman. But, again as in the western territories, these contests were largely organized by the priests of cities and provinces and regions. In the province of Asia (western Asia Minor), where there were schools at Smyrna (Izmir), Philadelphia (Alasehir), Cyzicus and Pergamum, Galen's service as gladiators' doctor took place under five successive high priests. These religious functionaries often maintained their own permanent troops of gladiators – some being their slaves, others bought from a predecessor, others again free men who had volunteered. Certain inscriptions, notably from Thasos and Trajana Augusta (Stara Zagora in Bulgaria), seem to refer to a 'high priest of arms', i.e. for gladiators, a phrase that has been interpreted to signify that at four-year intervals these Greek cities elected a priestly official who was expected, like the *quinquennales* elected every

4. A wild-beast hunt is also shown.

five years in western towns, to provide something particularly magnificent. At Sagalassus, now Aglasun in Asiatic
Turkey, we are told that the glory derived by the high
priest Tertullus both from his actions and from his ancestry
was much enhanced by a generous provision of wild-beast
hunts and gladiatorial displays, which showed, as the inscription rather crudely continues, 'that he preferred his
country to his financial position'. There is also record of the
priests' wives being associated with them in the presentation of these entertainments. As in many western regions,
so in the east, the practice was especially closely linked
with the provincial and municipal cult of emperors; the
walls of the Temple of Rome and Augustus at Ancyra
(Ankara) in Galatia bear a list of the liberalities of their
priests.

Semi-developed Galatia, like Pontus to its north, was
fond of this sport. But it was most popular at urban centres
such as Alexandria, with its own imperial gladiators'
school. However, the city from which the practice originally spread through the east was apparently the cosmo-
politan Romanized port and colony of Corinth. Apuleius
tells of one of its chief officials, Thiasus, who travelled
round Greece looking for gladiators and wild beasts.

Since convention required him to live up to the dignity of his
appointment by staging a public entertainment, he had undertaken to provide a three-day gladiatorial show in evidence of
his open-handedness. It was this, indeed, that accounted for his
presence in northern Greece: he was trying to please his fellow-
citizens by buying up the finest wild animals and hiring the
most famous gladiators in all Thessaly . . .

At an earlier date, the Roman governors of provinces had also been among those who could give such shows. But Nero prohibited the practice, on the grounds that 'this ostensible generosity had been as oppressive to financials as extortion, the governors' intention being to win partisans to screen their irregularities'. In about AD 200 it was also stipulated, for security reasons, that governors needed an imperial permit before they could transport gladiators outside their province. The emperors, in fact, were cautious and suspicious about allowing major gladiatorial activities to anyone of importance other than themselves. Another security measure is detectable in the frequent choice of islands, such as Thasos and Cos, as the residences of gladiators' troops.

GLADIATORS
IN ACTION

THE DIFFERENT KINDS OF GLADIATORS

It was from successive waves of prisoners of war conscript-
ed as gladiators that the profession inherited its bizarre,
exotic uniforms which were one of the sources of public
enjoyment. From Republican times onwards, foreign prisoners were made to fight with their own weapons and in
their own styles. Many of these men, it is true, were merely
wretched captives herded into the arena, but various
classes of professional gladiator likewise came from this
category. Such, for example, was the origin of the gladiators known as Samnites. Generally regarded as the prototypes of all Rome's gladiators, they are said to have come
into existence after its Samnite enemies introduced a splendid new type of military equipment in 310 BC.

In a battle two years later, they lost heavy casualties, and
the men of Campania – presumably Rome's Capuan allies
– captured a large quantity of their uniforms and arms.
Then, reports Livy, these Campanians 'equipped after this
fashion the gladiators who furnished them entertainment
at their feasts, and bestowed on them the name of Samnites'
The Romans adopted the same equipment when they insti-
tuted their first gladiatorial games in 264 BC. These 'Samnites' wore the heavy, magnificent armour of the soldiers

after whom they were designated. It included a large
oblong shield (*scutum*), a leather or partly metal greave
(*ocrea*) on the left leg, and a vizored helmet (*galea*) with
huge crest and plumes. To these were added sword (*gladius*)
or lance (*hasta*), and the sleeve on the right arm which was
part of a gladiator's general equipment. For a long time
these 'Samnites' were the only gladiators the Romans knew.

But then came other types of fighter with national names,
the 'Thracians' and 'Gauls'. Although the 'Thracians' were
an innovation of Sulla (d. 78 BC) and receive their first surviving literary reference from Cicero, and although according to one version the 'Gauls' were not introduced into
Rome until the time of Caesar's Gallic campaigns, the previous appearance of both types of fighter on Etruscan
grave-urns as early as the third century BC – two reliefs
show a Gaul against a Gaul, and one a Gaul against a
Thracian – indicate that in Etruria at least fighters of such
kinds were known at this more antique date. 'Thracians'
carried a curved scimitar (*sica*) of varying shape, and a
small square or round shield (*parma*). In addition to bands
of leather (*fasciae*) round their legs or thighs, they wore
not one greave, like the 'Samnites' (against whom they
sometimes fought), but two. These features are, for example, identifiable on a relief at Smyrna (Izmir) showing a
gladiator called Priscus, who is specifically described as
a 'Thracian'.

The Gaulish nation also long retained gladiators of its
own. *Trinqui* were sacrificial victims, *cruppellarii* wore
heavy cuirasses; fighters of this type were enrolled by
Gallic rebels against Rome in AD 21. The Roman gladiators
known as 'Gauls' belonged to a different category, which

may have come to Etruria from the Gaulish populations of north Italy (Cisalpine Gaul); and from there they probably passed to Rome via Etruscan Campania. In the imperial period 'Gauls' were gradually superseded by a type of gladiator known as the *myrmillo*, named after the representation of a sea-fish (*mormylos, mormyros*) which he wore in his helmet.

Another type of fighter at this later date was the *secutor* or chaser. It has been usual to regard the *secutores* as an offspring of the heavy-armoured 'Samnite',[1] but in the present state of our knowledge they cannot always readily be told apart from the 'Gaul' and *myrmillo*, or from another little known type called the *provocator* or challenger. Probably there was a good deal of diversity, within categories,[2] but by far the largest number of surviving representations of gladiators belong to a general, recognizable type which seems to cover the majority of the various classes. This typical fighter's torso and legs are usually, though not invariably, bare. He has a round or high vizored helmet (sometimes with a metal crest), a large rectangular or oval shield (unlike the small Thracian one), a dagger or short sword, and a greave on his left leg only (rarely on both): this completes for the left side of his body the protection afforded by his shield higher up, thus covering him from neck to knee. He wears a belt, sometimes a wide metal band but more often of leather, extending down to the

1. There were also successors of the 'Samnites' known as *hoplomachi*.

2. One complication is that, in the east, gladiatorial equipment continued to evolve; in the west, types mostly remained fixed, at least from AD 100 onwards.

thighs and covering the genitals. Leather bands (*manicae*) protect his exposed right arm that holds the dagger. Sometimes further bands are worn at the ankle, or calf, or above or below the knee or both, or round the thigh.

The *myrmillo* could fight against the 'Thracian' or against the *retiarius* or net-fighter. But the principal opponent of the latter was the *secutor*; it was to his pursuit of the *retiarius* that his name 'chaser' refers. This distinctive *retiarius* was provided with a trident or tunny-fish harpoon (*fascina*), a dagger, and a net to which a cord was fixed so that he could draw it back if it failed to ensnare his prey.[3] The head of the *retiarius* was, exceptionally, uncovered, except sometimes for a head-band. He wore a belt and leg-bands or ankle-bands, and his left shoulder was guarded by a leather or metal shoulder-piece (*galerus*). One of these *galeri* found at Pompeii is decorated with a crab, a dolphin and an anchor. These symbols recall that the *retiarius* was equipped after the manner of a fisherman; that is why a *myrmillo*, or fish-man, was a suitable adversary for him as an alternative to the *secutor*.

Although there may have been antique precedents for the throwing of a net as a method of combat, his lack of dignified armour (for which mobility was the substitute) meant that the unfortunate *retiarius* ranked as inferior in status, and was given the poorest living-quarters. When Juvenal is deploring the entrance of a descendant of the Gracchi into the amphitheatre, what makes it much worse is that he enrolls himself not in the less disreputable species

3. *Laquearii* were like *retiarii*, but employed a lasso instead of a net.

of heavy-armed gladiator but as a mere half-naked *retiarius*, rushing about the arena –

> The games! Go there for the ultimate scandal,
> Looking at Gracchus who fights, but not with the arms of a swordsman,
> Not with a dagger or shield (he hates and despises such weapons),
> Nor does a helmet hide his face. What he holds is a trident,
> What he hurls is a net, and he misses, of course, and we see him
> Look up at the seats, then run for his life, all around the arena,
> Easy for all to know and identify. Look at his tunic,
> Golden cord and fringe, and that queer conspicuous arm-guard!

There is, sometimes, a hint or analogy of homosexual exhibition; and in this connection it may be remarked that some gladiators assumed the names of famous pretty boys of mythology, Hylas, Narcissus and Hyacinthus, and that some of the admiring inscriptions set up in honour of gladiators seem to refer to male passions.

So probably a *retiarius* improved his status if he was also capable of fighting as a 'Samnite' – and such versatility was not uncommon. Yet *retiarii*, quite as much as other gladiators, are often depicted in every sort of artistic medium. A mosaic at Madrid shows one successfully enveloping the *secutor* in his net, and a Greek relief shows another on a platform fending off an opponent who stands below.

A further sort of gladiator is represented by the *andabatae*; their name was the title of one of Varro's lost satires, in the first century BC. Clad in chain-mail like oriental cavalry (*cataphracti*) and wearing vizored helmets without eye-holes, they charged blindly at one another on horseback. An encounter of this kind has been sketched on one of the walls of Pompeii's amphitheatre. Another type of gladiator, the *eques*, was likewise on horseback as his name suggests, wearing a tunic and carrying a round shield. *Velites* fought against one another on foot, each holding a spear with attached thong or strap (*hasta amentata*). *Essedarii*, probably introduced by Julius Caesar, charged at each other in horse-chariots after the British fashion, with a driver beside them. Martial tells of a female gladiator of this type; and a relief at Augusta Trevirorum (Trier) shows an *essedarius* chased by a panther. *Dimachaeri* were, as the word indicates, two-dagger men, unhelmeted. A relief from Amisus (Samsun) shows a pair engaged in combat. There were also *sagittarii* with bow and arrows fighting wild beasts and apparently other gladiators as well. An inscription records a further species of gladiators known as *scissores* (carvers), but we know little or nothing about them.

Usually fighters, of whatever kind, encountered each other in single combat, but multiple and mass duels were also frequent. One such incident, according to the gossip of Suetonius, elicited a peculiar version of sporting spirit from Caligula.

A group of net-and-trident *retiarii*, dressed in tunics, put up a very poor show against the five *secutores* with whom they were matched. But when the emperor sentenced them to death for cowardice, one of them seized a trident and killed each of his opponents in turn. Caligula then publicly expressed his horror at what he called 'this most bloody murder', and his disgust with those who had been able to stomach the sight.

Although faction partisanship was less vigorous in the arena than in the circus, there was quite strong feeling (accentuated by betting) in favour of one sort of gladiator against another. An inscription of the slave oil-dealer Crescens describes him as a Blue in the circus and a 'Thracian' in the amphitheatre. The emperor Caligula likewise favoured the 'Thracians', and trained as one himself.

He chose Thracian gladiators to officer his German bodyguard. On the other hand he reduced the defensive armour of the *myrmillones*; and when a gladiator of this sort, called Columbus, won a fight but was lightly wounded, Caligula treated him with a virulent poison which he afterwards called 'Columbinum' – at any rate that was how he described it in his catalogue of poisons.

Titus was another emperor who supported the 'Thracians'.

He took such pains to humour his subjects that, on one occasion, before a gladiatorial show, he promised to forgo his own preferences and let the audience choose what they liked best; and kept his word by refusing no request and encouraging everyone to tell him what each wanted. Yet he openly acknowledged his partisanship of the Thracian school of gladiators, and would gesture and argue vociferously with the crowd on this subject, though never losing either his dignity or his sense of justice.

On the other hand Titus' brother Domitian showed a disconcertingly violent backing for the *myrmillones*, with dire results for those who preferred the 'Thracians'. 'Domitian was always down on the Thracians and a chance remark by one citizen, to the effect that a Thracian gladiator might be "a match for the *myrmillo* who was his opponent, but not for the patron of the Games", was enough to have him dragged from his seat and – with a placard tied around his neck reading: "A Thracian supporter who spoke evil of his emperor" – torn to pieces by dogs in the arena.'

Marcus Aurelius claimed to be impartial in such matters, in accordance with the advice once given him by his tutor Fronto – 'who dissuaded me from patronizing Green or Blue at the races, or Light or Heavy in the amphitheatre'.

THE PROCEDURE OF THE ARENA

Gladiatorial shows were intensively advertised. Descriptions of forthcoming contests, written in colours by a special class of scribe, appeared on walls and on the gravestones beside main roads. Two such stones discovered outside Pompeii display announcements of games at Nola and Nuceria (Nocera). Numerius Festus Ampliatus of Pompeii declares that the whole world adores his troops of gladiators: they are *totius orbis desiderium*. Similar notices have come to light in the Balkans for example, at Thessalonica (Salonica), Serdica (Sofia) and Nicopolis ad Istrum (Nicupe). To maintain public interest, stop-press supplements, announcing new pairs of fighters, were added to the advertisements day by day. Then the lists were copied out, sold in the streets, and distributed. Heralds, too, were mobilized to cry out the names of prospective combatants, and men carried about banners proclaiming the same information in large letters. There were also programmes; Ovid, interested in the amphitheatre's opportunities for love-making, suggested the borrowing of a programme as a good way to strike up an acquaintance.

The grisly magnificence and ceremonial began upon the

day before the fights. For it was then that the giver of the show donated a splendid feast to the contestants about to appear on the following day. Hysterical scenes are recorded, and some of the 'free' volunteers among the performers used the macabre occasion to liberate their own slaves. The public were admitted to the dinner so that they could see with their own gloating eyes that nothing was being skimped. 'The curious', according to Carcopino,

circulated round the tables with unwholesome joy. Some of the guests, brutalized or fatalistic, abandoned themselves to the pleasures of the moment and ate gluttonously. Others, anxious to increase their chances by taking thought for their health, resisted the temptations of the generous fare and ate with moderation. The most wretched, haunted by a presentiment of approaching death, their throats and bellies already paralysed by fear, gave way to lamentation . . .

Greek fighters, we are told, took leave of their friends at these dinners, while Thracians and Celts were inclined to gorge heavily.

The proceedings of the murderous day itself began with a chariot-drive and parade. Led and presented by the sponsor of the games, the duellists displayed themselves in uniforms topped by cloaks dyed purple and covered with gold embroidery (a fragment of such a robe has been found at Pompeii). Climbing down from their chariots, they marched round the arena, followed by slaves carrying their arms and armour. Gladiators, especially those who belonged to the emperor's own troop, were often finely equipped. For example an embossed vizor-helmet, among several found at Pompeii, is superb, and the plumes on such helmets sometimes came from peacocks or ostriches. Julius Caesar

furnished his fighters with weapons covered with silver.
After the assassination of the emperor-gladiator Commodus,
the auction sale of his weapons included specimens studded
with jewels and precious stones.

When the combatants arrived opposite the emperor's
platform, they extended their right hands towards him
and cried 'Hail, emperor, greetings from men about to die!'
(*Ave, imperator, morituri te salutant!*) The terms of this
famous salute are recorded by Suetonius from the sham sea-
fight given by Claudius on the Fucine Lake. He adds, however, that the emperor spoilt the effect by calling back,
'Or not!' This example of his particularly fatuous humour
caused a momentary hitch, since the men thereupon re-
fused to fight, insisting that his words had excused them
and amounted to an imperial pardon.

Claudius grew so angry that he was on the point of sending
troops to massacre them all, or burning them in their ships.
However, he changed his mind, jumped from his throne and,
hobbling ridiculously down to the lakeside, threatened and
coaxed the gladiators into battle.

Staged with a dramatic sense of climax, the shows started
with second-rate warming-up displays that were bloodless.
One type of such exercise was provided by mock fighters
called *paegniarii*. A mosaic found at Nennig in Germany
shows one of them carrying a stick and his opponent brandishing a whip, and four such imitation combatants appear
on a monument from Amiternum. Occasionally they fought
during the slack time in the middle of the day, but more
often they provided an *hors d'oeuvre*. Caligula thought it
comic to mobilize as *paegniarii* respectable family men

1. Boxers, with their metal-weighted gloves and leather arm-strips, were familiar figures in the arena. This Roman mosaic, recently in the Lateran Museum (now being rearranged), was found in the Baths of Caracalla.

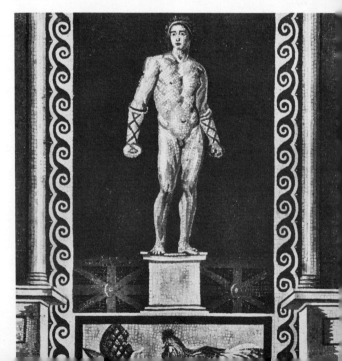

2. Funerary epitaph for two gladiators, fourth/fifth century AD (Benevento, Museo del Sannio).

3. This young boxer is depicted in a floor mosaic found in Pompeii (Rome, Museo Nazionale Romano).

4. Three statuettes of gladiators (the one shown on the left is in Naples, Museo Nazionale; the other two are in Paris, Bibliothèque Nationale).

5. *left* Two tomb-reliefs of gladiators from Izmir (Smyrna), Turkey. This Italian institution spread rapidly in the east, despite protests.

6. *right* Reliefs of gladiatorial combat.

7. *left* Three statuettes of
gladiators with different
weapons.

8. *right* An oil-lamp in the
form of a gladiatorial helmet
(Rome, Museo Artistico
Industriale).

9. *below* A first-century relief
of a gladiator (Benevento,
Museo del Sannio).

10. *above* This bronze sculpture of a retiarius (fighter with a trident and net), found at Esbarres (Côte-d'Or), is in Paris, Bibliothèque Nationale.

11. *above right* This gladiatorial dress helmet found at Pompeii is decorated in high relief (Naples, Museo Nazionale).

12. *below right* Relief of animal combat (Rome, Museo Torlonia).

13. An elaborate bronze greave (armour for lower leg) and three bronze gladiatorial helmets with relief decoration (all at Naples, Museo Nazionale).

14. This fresco, now preserved in Naples, Museo Nazionale, shows riots between the men of Pompeii and Nuceria in and around the amphitheatre at Pompeii in AD 59.

15. Two brass coins, minted in the time of Titus and in the third century, show views of the Roman Colosseum.

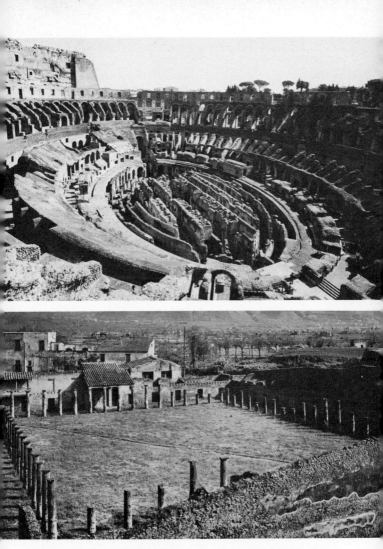

16. *top* The interior of the Colosseum in Rome. This picture shows the cells and passages (originally covered by the arena) used for the organization of the spectacles and the housing of wild beasts.

17. *bottom* The gladiatorial barracks – apparently also a training-school – at Pompeii.

18. *below* The amphitheatre of Pompeii. It accommodated twenty thousand spectators – many for a smallish town.

19. *above right* The Roman amphitheatre in Nîmes. The French king François I was greatly impressed by these remains.

20. *below right* The Roman amphitheatre in Arles. In the Middle Ages two thousand people lived in this building.

21. Two parts of a fourth-century mosaic of gladiatorial combats. The individual combatants are identified by name (both at Rome, Galleria Borghese).

22. *above* This stele of a gladiator comes from Ephesus; now in Turkey (cast in Berlin).

23. *right* Two mosaics of gladiatorial combats (Augst near Basel [Augusta Rauricorum] Museum).

24. *left* A fragment of a first-century relief of a gladiator (Benevento, Museo del Sannio).

25. *below* Drawings of gladiators from Pompeii walls.

27. A fourth-
century mosaic
of gladiatorial
combats: supreme
monument of bad
taste (Rome,
Galleria Borghese).

26. Detail of fourth-century Roman mosaics of animal hunting in the arena.

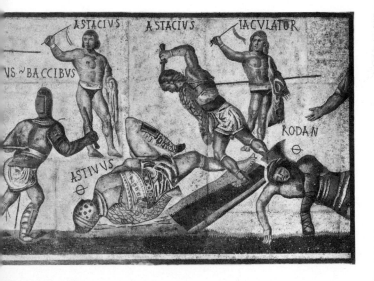

28. Reliefs of gladiatorial
combats
left Rome, Museo Nuovo
Capitolino.
below Rome, Museo
Nazionale Romano.

29. *right* The prelude to a
gladiatorial execution.

30. *Graffiti* of animal combats. The one above was found in the
Colosseum in Rome. The one on the right is from Pompeii.

31. *left* This Roman sarcophagus is decorated with a relief of gladiators (Aquila, Museo Nazionale d'Abruzzo).

32. *below* Fourth-century Roman mosaic of animal hunting.

33. Roman terracotta oil-lamps with reliefs of gladiators (all at
Rome, Museo Nazionale Romano).

34. This funeral stele of a gladiator is preserved in Milan, Museo d'Arte Antica, Castello Sforzesco.

who happened to be crippled by some conspicuous bodily deformity. A second type of preliminary fighter, the *lusorii*, utilized the technique of gladiators but employed wooden weapons. Their displays were called *prolusiones*, or *lusiones* when, as sometimes happened, they occupied a whole day or days.

When *paegniarii* or *lusorii* had whetted spectators' appetites, the serious fighters were chosen by lot and in public, as a demonstration that all was above board. From now on the weapons were sharp and dangerous, and the giver of the games had to conduct a testing ceremony in order to confirm that this was so.[4] One brand of sword was named after Tiberius' son Drusus, who liked them particularly well-sharpened. So did Domitian, and his court poet Martial celebrated the revival of the 'simpler' antique custom of truly lethal, cut-throat swords.

The first fight with sharp weapons was announced by the sombre strains of the war-trumpet (*tuba*). Then, during the fights, there were further blasts upon trumpets and upon horns, and the shriller screams and trills of pipes and flutes. Reliefs on gladiatorial monuments show a hydraulic organ, and there were probably singers also. Some form or other of musical accompaniment may well have continued throughout the spectacle.

While the fighters were at grips, their trainers stood beside them and hounded them on. With these were slaves holding leather straps (*lorarii*), which they used at the trainer's bidding to lash any insufficiently vigorous performers, or they even goaded him on with red-hot irons.

4. Sharp weapons: *arma decretoria*. Testing ceremony: *probatio armorum*.

Meanwhile the crowd shouted training-manual slogans and directions, varied by ferocious injunctions to flog, and kill, and burn.

When a man fell, the heralds raised their trumpets, and spectators yelled 'Got him! He's had it!' (*habet, hoc habet*). The fallen fighter, if he was in a state to move, laid down his shield, and raised one finger of his left hand as a plea for mercy. The decision whether his life should be spared rested with the provider of the games; but he generally found it politic to take account of the spectators' loudly expressed views. According to one familiar tradition, thumbs up (accompanied by a waving of handkerchiefs) meant that the man should be spared, thumbs down that he should not, and a relief seems to show the former gesture indicating mercy. The Latin terms, however (*vertere, premere pollicem*), might seem to suggest the contrary conclusion, the upward gesture imitating the fatal weapon and the downward one directing that the weapon should be thrown down. The answer must still be regarded as uncertain. At all events Roman onlookers were hard on a gladiator who seemed to value his life too highly. 'Take warning from my fate!' says a pathetic epitaph. 'No quarter for the fallen, whoever he may be!'

Indeed, spectators were extremely critical of any performance that did not come up to the mark. Petronius tells of Trimalchio's guest Echion who had unfriendly things to say about a show recently given by a certain Norbanus.

After all, what good has Norbanus done us? He put on some half-pint gladiators, so done in already that they'd have dropped if you blew at them. I've seen animal-killers fight better. As for the horsemen killed, he got them off a lamp – they ran round like cocks in a backyard. One was just a cart-horse, the other couldn't stand up, and the reserve was just one corpse instead of another – he was practically hamstrung. One boy did have a bit of spirit – he was in Thracian armour, and even he didn't show any initiative. In fact, they were all flogged afterwards, there were so many shouts of 'Give 'em what for!' from the crowd. Pure yellow, that's all. 'Well, I've put on a show for you,' he says. 'And I'm clapping you,' says I. 'Reckon it up – I'm giving more than I got. So we're quits.'

These unsatisfactory fighters were fortunate to get off with a beating. For century after century tens of thousands of others, throughout the empire, did not leave the amphitheatres alive. Byron was moved to picture one such victim – a prisoner of war from a remote village of Dacia.

> The arena swims around him – he is gone,
> Ere ceased the inhuman shout which hailed the wretch who won.
> He heard it, but he heeded not – his eyes
> Were with his heart, and that was far away;
> He recked not of the life he lost nor prize,
> But where his rude hut by the Danube lay,
> There were his young barbarians all at play,
> There was their Dacian mother – he, their sire,
> Butchered to make a Roman holiday.

While African boys raked over the bloodstained sand, fallen gladiators were taken away. A ghoulish touch, reminiscent of the religious origins of the sport, was added by the costumes worn by those who removed the bodies, who were dressed as Mercury (Hermes Psychopompos), divine guide of dead men's souls to the infernal regions. Another distasteful note was struck by officials disguised as

Charon; for when a man had been struck down and lay in his death agony, it was the function of these Charons to finish him off. The slaughtered men were carried out through the Porta Libitinensis, named after Libitina the goddess of burials.

After the killing was over, careful lists were made of what had taken place. Some of these have survived: they show the combatants' names followed by the fateful letters P (*eriit*), perished, V (*icit*), won, or M (*issus*), a loser who was allowed to survive to fight another day. For these *missi* were spared; they left the arena by a special Porta Sanavivaria. Some impresarios eager to make generous response to the crowd's bloodthirsty tastes boasted of allowing no *missio*: that is to say they were proud to have had all the losers killed. But Augustus, though lavish with the lives of gladiators, restrained Nero's haughty, extravagant grandfather from still persisting with this practice even after he had been confidentially warned to give it up. Such decisions, of course, often rested with the emperor himself, as the most conspicuous member of the crowd and the principal holder of games. In a nastily sycophantic poem Martial poured praises upon Domitian – not usually regarded as a mild man – for finally calling a halt when there was a deadlock, and saving the lives of both contestants.

> Priscus and Verus fought in equal strife;
> Long time in level balance hung their life;
> For their dismissal many a shout was made;
> But the just monarch his own law obeyed.
> Still must they fight and lay the shield aside;
> Viands and gifts he gave them, nought beside.

At last the struggle found an issue fair,
And equal victory and defeat they share.
To both were freedom and the palm assigned;
Such recompense did skill and valour find.
Who, Caesar, else but then the law laid down
That two could merit, two receive the crown?

Trajan too, on another occasion, apparently let all the contestants go.

If a fighter's performance had not given satisfaction, or if he was a criminal whose survival was not desired, his life was sometimes hazarded again on the same day by orders for a repeat performance, against specially introduced substitutes or understudies (*suppositicii, tertiarii*). But it was regarded as unsporting of Caracalla (AD 211–217) to bring on two successive substitutes against a single fighter Bato, who was thus forced to engage in three successive duels on a single day. This was plain murder – which the emperor enjoyed – and the third time Bato was killed. However, Caracalla honoured him with a brilliant funeral.

When neither party won and both were spared, each was described as *stans missus*, and such a result is often recorded on inscriptions. The epitaph of the gladiator Flamma, who lived to the age of thirty, records that he won twenty-five contests, was *missus* four times, and *stans missus* nine times. But there were possible pitfalls, and pathetic complaints about stabs in the back: at Amisus (Samsun) a fighter called Diodorus is made to assert posthumously, on his funerary relief, that he was killed by a treacherous blow after he had won his fight.

The victorious gladiators were presented with palm branches as a prize, and in Greek lands of the empire they were given a wreath or crown in addition or instead. Both palms and crowns are often shown on funeral monuments; a certain Faustus claims to have received as many as thirty-seven crowns. The giver of the games also provided prize-money, according to scales stipulated in the gladiators' contracts. Marcus Aurelius fixed maximum rates, based on the purchase prices of individual fighters; the monetary reward was limited to one-fifth of this price in the case of a slave, one-quarter for a free man. After the performance, these prizes were doled out to the victorious duellists in front of the public, who joined vociferously in the counting. At a supplementary show which he called 'the picnic', the emperor Claudius himself entered into the fun while distributing the rewards. Cracking jokes and urging the spectators to enjoy themselves, he vulgarly exposed his left hand – instead of keeping it decently covered by his gown – and counted the number of gold pieces aloud on his fingers as he did so. On such occasions the coins were heaped up in valuable bowls, which went with them as part of the gift. Moreover, there were occasional possibilities of more sensational windfalls: Nero presented the *myrmillo* Spiculus (a lyre-player as well) with properties and residences as valuable as those that went to generals who had earned Triumphs for their victories.

THE ARENAS

In early times gladiators' duels took place in whatever public spaces a town might possess. But then, under the emperors, the characteristic scene for such contests was the amphitheatre. This was an oval auditorium surrounded by rows of seats facing on to the 'arena' or sand, which, as in modern bull-rings, filled the elliptical central area, absorbing the blood of slaughtered men and beasts. Caligula and Nero, however, favoured coloured dusts instead of sand – white and greenish-blue (copper) dust, and red minium.

The first permanent amphitheatre known to us is not in Rome but in Campania, the country which was particularly devoted to gladiatorial games and may have passed them on to the Romans. This is the amphitheatre at Pompeii – though an even more prominent Campanian centre of gladiatorship, Capua, probably had an older one, subsequently superseded by the much larger buildings of which something can be seen today – the largest (together with those at another Campanian town, Puteoli) of which we have any knowledge until the Colosseum was built at Rome. The Pompeii structure, which dates from soon after 80 BC, was an enormous one for a not very large town, its seating capacity ultimately rising to 20,000 places. Dug deep into the earth with a low frontage and external steps which lead up to the top of the auditorium, it recalls that in earlier times these arenas had been natural hollows with heaped-up earth round their circumference.

In the reign of Nero, this Pompeian amphitheatre was the scene of a violent brawl between the people of Pompeii and the inhabitants of its neighbour Nuceria, now Nocera (AD 59). Their feud, which showed just how savage, under the surface tranquillity of the *pax Romana*, such rivalries could become, was kept alive by partisan *graffiti* still visible on the walls of Pompeii, and the incident itself is depicted in a wall-painting from the same town which gives an interesting bird's-eye view of the amphitheatre itself and of the rioting. Tacitus indicates how seriously the disturbance was taken by the authorities at Rome.

It arose out of a trifling incident at a gladiatorial show given by a man who had been expelled from the Roman senate, Livineius Regulus. During an exchange of taunts – characteristic of these disorderly country towns – abuse led to stone-throwing, and then swords were drawn. The people of Pompeii, where the show was held, came off best. Many wounded and mutilated Nucerians were taken to the capital. Many bereavements, too, were suffered by parents and children. The emperor instructed the senate to investigate the affair; and the senate passed it to the consuls. When they reported back, the senate debarred Pompeii from holding any similar gathering for ten years. Illegal associations in the town were dissolved; and Livineius and his fellow-instigators of the disorders were exiled.

This Pompeii amphitheatre, in gladiator-loving Campania, had antedated any Roman counterpart by half a century. In the capital, the earliest duels took place in the markets and then at the Forum Romanum, in which temporary stands were erected for the spectators. As late as the time of Augustus, the rather conservative architectural expert Vitruvius advises designers of forums to bear in mind the requirements of such displays.

However, by that date Rome had already seen its first arenas. For in 53 BC – the very year, incidentally, in which the first stone theatre was built in the capital – the young politician Gaius Scribonius Curio, a friend of Julius Caesar's, erected a wooden amphitheatre.[5] According to Pliny the

5. Caesar built another in 46 BC.

elder, it consisted of two hemicyclical theatres built back to back. He adds that they were equipped with a pivot mechanism enabling the pair of buildings, when gladiatorial and wild-beast shows were required, to be converted into a single elliptical amphitheatre. The nature of this mechanical device has been much disputed; but Pliny (or the source of his information) may have made the whole thing up, in a mistaken effort to explain how the word 'amphitheatre' came to be invented. But meanwhile, before he wrote, the earliest permanent structure of this kind had been erected at Rome by Augustus' henchman Titus Statilius Taurus, whose family may well have possessed its own gladiatorial school near by. Taurus' building (29 BC) was probably destroyed in the Great Fire of Nero's reign. It was partly made of stone, and partly of wood.

Wooden amphitheatres were highly dangerous, and from time to time throughout Roman imperial history they collapsed. Tacitus gives a graphic account of such a catastrophe at Fidenae, just north of Rome, during the reign of Tiberius (AD 27). 'As destructive,' he says,

as a major war, it began and ended in a moment. An ex-slave called Atilius started building an amphitheatre at Fidenae for a gladiatorial show. But he neither rested its foundations on solid ground nor fastened the wooden superstructure securely. He had undertaken the project not because of great wealth or municipal ambition but for sordid profits. Lovers of such displays, starved of amusements under Tiberius, flocked in – men and women of all ages. Their numbers, swollen by the town's proximity, intensified the tragedy. The packed structure collapsed, subsiding both inwards and outwards and precipitating or overwhelming a huge crowd of spectators and bystanders.

Those killed at the outset of the catastrophe at least escaped torture, as far as their violent deaths permitted. More pitiable were those, mangled but not yet dead, who knew their wives and children lay there too. In daytime they could see them, and at night they heard their screams and moans. The news attracted crowds, lamenting kinsmen, brothers, and fathers. Even those whose friends and relations had gone away on other business were alarmed, for while the casualties remained un-identified uncertainty gave free range for anxieties. When the ruins began to be cleared, people rushed to embrace and kiss the corpses – and even quarrelled over them, when features were unrecognizable but similarities of physique or age had caused wrong identifications.

Fifty thousand people were mutilated or crushed to death in the disaster. The senate decreed that in future no one with a capital of less than four hundred thousand sesterces should ex-hibit a gladiatorial show, and no amphitheatre should be con-structed except on ground of proved solidity. Atilius was banished. Immediately after the catastrophe, leading Romans threw open their homes, providing medical attention and sup-plies all round. In those days Rome, for all its miseries, recalled the practice of our ancestors, who after great battles had lavished gifts and attentions on the wounded.

The next emperor, Caligula, characteristically expressed regret that in his own reign no interesting disaster like that of Fidenae had occurred. Certain later rulers could not say the same, since wooden buildings of this kind continued to fall down, for example under Antoninus Pius when 1,112 lives were lost, and again a hundred and fifty years later.

Yet by then great stone amphitheatres had been in existence for centuries. Nero, in addition to erecting a wooden one in the Campus Martius, laid the foundations for an imposing edifice of stone. Soon afterwards, on the site of a lake in the grounds of what had been that emperor's Golden House, the largest and most famous of all such buildings was initiated by the Flavian dynasty. Opened by Titus in AD 80, this Colosseum, which takes its name from the colossal statue of Nero that stood close by, is, for all its horrific purpose, one of the most marvellous buildings in the world. Its massive overall measurements are 187 by 155 metres, of which the space for the arena itself comprises 86 by 54. There was accommodation for perhaps 45,000 sitting spectators and 5,000 more standing. They reached their places through 76 numbered entrance arches out of the 80 that pierced the exterior; two of the others were reserved for the emperor and his entourage; and two for gladiatorial processions. Underneath the arena is a honeycomb of passages for stage effects, cells for wild beasts, rooms for storage, and the site of the mechanism by which scenery and other apparatus were hoisted into the arena.[6]

The emperor's platform was at the centre of one of the long sides, facing across to the portion of the auditorium reserved for magistrates and the holder of the games. There were also places for priests and Vestal Virgins, whose traditional prominent position at entertainments included attendance at these bloodthirsty sports. Places were also set aside for imperial ladies, and for kings and delegates of foreign peoples. Foreigners were also amply represented in

6. The present substructures mainly date from a rebuilding in late antiquity. The emperor's platform was called the *pulvinar*, and the place for the holder of the games the *tribunal editoris*.

the less distinguished seats. According to the ruler-worshipping ecstasies of Martial,

> Each Arab, each Sabaean comes this way,
> Cilicians wet with their own saffron spray;
> The fierce Sugambrian with braided hair,
> Aethiops with knotted tresses hither fare,
> With voices manifold but one accord
> To hail their country's father and its lord!

The vast crowds sweltering in the upper sectors of the amphitheatre were sometimes protected by a huge awning, supported by a mast or masts which sailors drew across the entire circumference. At one of Nero's shows the awning was studded with stars.

The curving exteriors of Greek theatres had normally displayed two storeys of arcades. Under Augustus, at Rome, this had been exceeded by the three-tier stone Theatre of Marcellus. In its final form the Colosseum was extended upwards to four storeys. The arches penetrating the three nearest to the ground rest upon piers to which are attached three-quarter columns of the Doric, Ionic and Corinthian Orders respectively. The topmost tier is not arcaded: like those beneath, it exhibits the Greek Orders but here they take the form of rectangular engaged columns (pilasters) with Corinthian capitals. Yet these classical Orders are only there to give scale and ornamentation. The essential constructional units are the massive arch-bearing piers, which thus supply an organic link between exterior and interior.

The cumulation of these arches one above another to this unprecedented height of four storeys was made possible by the epoch-making invention of concrete. A masterpiece of construction such as the Colosseum shows how such concrete-cored arches, needed to give maximum efficiency to the gladiatorial auditorium, could also be exploited for impressive ornamental effect. Here is a significant development of that other Roman invention of the single or triple Triumphal Arch: namely the arcade, a great row of arches forming a single composition.

These almost interminably repeated arcades show in its most majestic form the instinctive Italian capacity for dramatic presentation. The architecture of the Romans includes great religious monuments, too, but their vast amphitheatres provide a reminder that, unlike the same art among the Greeks, it was also, to at least as great an extent, secular; though its description, for that reason, as an architecture of humanism requires some qualifications when the appalling purposes of these magnificent structures are recalled.[7]

For the building is still replete with a potent, ineradicable impression of evil. Benvenuto Cellini tells how he conducted spiritualistic experiments in the Colosseum. For it was here, in what Byron calls this 'noble wreck in ruinous perfection', that

> Murder breathed her bloody steam;
> And here, where buzzing nations choked the ways,
> And roared or murmured like a mountain stream
> Dashing or winding as its torrent strays,
> Here, where the Roman million's blame or praise
> Was death or life, the playthings of a crowd ...
> But when the rising moon begins to climb
> Its topmost arch, and gently pauses there;
> When the stars twinkle through the loops of time,

7. *The World of Rome*, pp. 274-6.

> And the low night-breeze waves along the air
> The garland-forest, which the gray walls wear,
> Like laurels on the bald first Caesar's head;
> When the light shines serene but doth not glare,
> Then in this magic circle raise the dead;
> Heroes have trod this spot – 'tis on their dust ye tread.

Heroes have trod the spot, and other good, too, has come out of evil, for it is undeniable that the horrors of the gladiatorial shows produced one of the most magnificent architectural inventions and achievements of all time.

Nor has any other building anywhere exercised such far-reaching effects. The formula of the Colosseum helped to mould Renaissance styles. Together with the Theatre of Marcellus, it influenced Michelangelo's courtyard of the Palazzo Farnese in the same city; and before that it had inspired the façade of one of the earliest important Roman palaces, the Palazzo della Cancelleria of Andrea Bregno (Montecavallo) and Bramante (1483–1511); aptly enough, both palaces, like other buildings before them, were actually made of stones from the Colosseum.[8] Its communications-system also contributed the method of design which gave the palaces of Italy and Europe their staircases. Moreover, a profound influence was exercised by the brick ribs of its barrel-vaulting, one of the earliest instances of this structural form.

Of the Colosseum they said in the eighth century, 'As long as it stands, Rome will stand; when it falls, Rome will fall; when Rome falls, the world will fall.' The Colosseum has often been raided, but has never fallen. It has been made to serve manifold purposes. These have included

8. Poggio Bracciolini unavailingly complained of these plunderings.

sacred occasions – church services, Passion Plays, Capuchin sermons to destitute women; and it has provided housing accommodation for hermits. Like so many of its counterparts in other places, the Colosseum is solid enough to defy all manner of depredations, and this virtually indestructible building still towers over the city today.

Ranging down in size from the immensity of the Colosseum, more than seventy similar structures have been identified in other regions of the Roman empire, and probably there were many more. To begin with, there was an abundant series of arenas of all sizes in every part of Italy. At Rome itself, an amphitheatre for the praetorian guard (*castrense*) seems to go back to the third-century emperors Elagabalus or Severus Alexander. With an arena of 38 × 25 metres, this three-storey structure displayed the characteristic late imperial fashion of brick facings and pilasters. The walled-up arcades of the lowest tier are visible today, and it can be seen how they were incorporated into the city-wall by Honorius (d. 423).

Elsewhere in Italy, Pompeii and Capua have already been mentioned. The corresponding building at Verona, described in Merovingian times as a labyrinth and employed in the later Middle Ages for duels and executions, still retains nearly the whole of its stone seats but only four bays of the outside walls. Conversely at Pola (Pula, now in Yugoslavia), where the amphitheatre holding 22,000 spectators was long believed to have been built by superhuman hands, its outside walls have survived, but not the seats; rather as at Pompeii, there are four projecting bays containing open arcades and staircases. Casinum (S. Germano) is peculiar for the possession of an arena that is not elliptical but round. Augusta Praetoria (Aosta) exceptionally places its amphitheatre inside the walls – usually in such towns they were outside – probably for reasons of security, since the mountains and their tribesmen were not far away. At Sutrium (Sutri) in Etruria the seats, corridors and arena were all cut out of the solid rock. Ostia is a mystery; there is a late reference to an amphitheatre, but no trace of it has been found. Album Intimilium (Ventimiglia) has a very small building (35 × 31 metres), proportionate to the town's modest size. At Catana (Catania in Sicily) the amphitheatre was preserved under a layer of lava. At a number of Italian sites, large tasks of excavation still remain to be undertaken.

The pattern was reduplicated throughout the empire, in every conceivable variation and size; though the dimensions often depended more on the money available than on population figures. 'In some instances,' observes Sir Mortimer Wheeler, 'earthen banks enclosing an oval space and supplemented by timbering or a little masonry were regarded as adequate. Even a legionary fortress like Deva (Chester), which eventually had a fine stone structure, might begin with a timber amphitheatre, put up by the garrison in the first days of occupation just as its modern military successors might hastily improvise a football-ground.'

Army amphitheatres in the provinces included those at Lambaesis in Numidia, built by Trajan (arena 38 × 25 metres), and Carnuntum (Petronell) beside the Danube (98 × 75), where the building was enlarged by degrees, furnished with an enclosed box for official spectators, and shored up by columns on the long river side. Aquincum (Budapest), like Rome, had both a military and a civilian arena. But in general throughout the empire far the greater number of such structures were intended for the civilian populations. Some were tiny, such as the building at Cimiez, holding at first 500–600 and later 3,000 spectators. On the other hand Arelate (Arles) and Nemausus (Nîmes) have particularly imposing two-storey amphitheatres. The Arelate example (136 × 108 metres, arena 69 × 39) with three defensive towers, was in medieval times inhabited by 2,000 people speaking a dialect of their own. Nemausus has an amphitheatre (132 × 101 metres, arena 69 × 39) dating from Augustus with a heavy lintel construction reminiscent of wooden prototypes; the remains profoundly impressed François I. Their counterpart at Forum Julii (Fréjus) was massive enough to stand up to the breach of the Reyran dam in 1959. At Augusta Trevirorum (Trier), near the frontier, the three-tiered amphitheatre served as a fortified point. Many such ruins, large or small, fascinated later generations into creating legends around them; the surviving fragments at Burdigala (Bordeaux) and Limonum (Poitiers) were known as Palais Galliennes, after a Moorish princess beloved by Charlemagne.

Emerita in Lusitania (Mérida, W. Spain) had an amphitheatre dug out of the centre of a small hall. A town as remote as Caesarea in Mauretania (Cherchel) boasted an arena measuring 140 by 60 metres, a good deal longer than that of the Colosseum. At Thysdrus (El Djem in Tunisia) Gordian III (AD 238–44) began to build an amphitheatre with 64 arches of exceptionally wide intercolumniation.

The masonry, of local stone, is of first-class quality, but the building was never completed.

Verulamium (St Albans), like Lutetia Parisiorum (Paris) and a good many other places of modest size in Gaul and Germany, employed a formula which combined the functions of amphitheatre and theatre. At some towns in the eastern provinces, on the other hand, theatres were overlaid and superseded by amphitheatres, as an increasingly brutalized and Romanized taste demanded more numerous or ambitious gladiatorial displays and wild-beast hunts. This happened, for example, at Dodona in Epirus and Xanthus (Kinik) in Asia Minor. The erroneous view that gladiators were not favoured in Greek-speaking regions was largely based on the fact that a few Hellenic or Hellenized philosophers protested against them. But their objections, which will be described elsewhere, neither reflected nor influenced popular demand, which, in the orient as in the west, came to want this type of carnage and got it.

In Greece and the east, gladiatorial spectacles were occasionally given in stadiums, more often in theatres. There were also temporary amphitheatres, for instance at Antioch in Pisidia (Yalvaç). But quite a number of towns possessed permanent structures. These included, for example, Corinth in Greece; Gortyna in Crete; Antioch (Antakya) and Berytus (Beirut) in Syria-Phoenicia; Caesarea (Sdot Yam) in Palestine; Pergamum (Bergama), Cyzicus, Nysa (Sultanhisar) and perhaps Laodicea ad Lycum in Asia Minor; and Dura-Europos as far away as Mesopotamia. At Alexandria in Egypt recent excavations have unearthed a complete amphitheatre under a rubbish-heap next to the mosque of Nabi Danial. Athens also, in spite of opposition from a few of its more high-minded citizens, provided gladiatorial combats. Indeed they even staged them in the revered building where the great tragedians had seen their plays performed – the Theatre of Dionysus beside the Acropolis.

THE SEA-FIGHTS

One of the most extravagant forms of combat was the *naumachia* or naval battle. Huge areas were flooded in order to make artificial lakes for the ships, and gladiators, especially prisoners of war, were trained to fight on board.

The first of these large-scale sea-fights was organized by Julius Caesar upon a lake specially created in the Campus Martius at Rome. The rival fleets consisted of ships of various types carrying 1,000 sailors and 2,000 oarsmen, got up to represent the navies of Egypt and Tyre. As Suetonius remarks of the triumphal entertainments on that occasion, 'such huge numbers of visitors flocked to these shows that many of them had to sleep in tents pitched along the streets or roads, or on rooftops: and often the pressure of the crowd crushed people to death. The victims included two senators.'

After Caesar's death the area was filled in owing to the insanitary smells which it exhaled, but Augustus dug a huge pit beside the right bank of the Tiber so that this sort of entertainment could continue. The pit measured 557 by 536 metres – three times the size of the Colosseum – and was filled up with water broken by a man-made island and fringed by thickets and parks. Here, to celebrate the dedication of the Temple of Mars the Avenger in Caesar's honour, Augustus organized a naval battle between 'Athenians and Persians' (2 BC). Not counting oarsmen, as many as 6,000 gladiators took part. Ovid saw the occasion as a record-breaking opportunity for ecumenical assignations.

> The other morn in mimic fight
>   We saw a Grecian fleet arrayed,
> While Persian galleys painted bright
>   Their part as fierce assailants played ...
>
> From every land fair maidens came
>   And youths from every sea around,
> Abundant fuel for love's flame,
>   When all the world in Rome was found.
> Each manly heart was in a whirl
> Enraptured by some foreign girl.

But the greatest gladiatorial water-fight of all time was provided by Claudius to celebrate the completion of his tunnel through the mountains from the Fucine Lake in the Abruzzi to the River Liris (Garigliano). Sailing upon the lake in their triremes and quadriremes, the combatants adopted the roles of Sicilian and Rhodian fighters and sailors. The signal for their engagement was a trumpet-blast sounded by a silver Triton diving up from the depths of the waters.

Claudius had equipped warships manned with nineteen thousand combatants, surrounding them with a circle of rafts to prevent their escape. Enough space in the middle, however, was left for energetic rowing, skilful steering, charging, and all the incidents of a sea-battle ... The coast, the slopes, and the hill-tops were thronged like a theatre by innumerable spectators, who had come from the neighbouring towns and even from

Rome itself – to see the show or pay respects to the emperor. Claudius presided in a splendid military cloak, with Agrippina in a mantle of cloth of gold. Though the fighters were criminals they fought like brave men. After much blood-letting, they were spared extermination.

When the display was over, the waterway was opened. But careless construction became evident. The tunnel had not been sunk to the bottom of the lake or even half-way down; and so the channel was deepened. When this had been done, a second crowd was assembled, this time to witness an infantry battle fought by gladiators on pontoons. But, to the horror of banqueters near the lake's outlet, the force of the out-rushing water swept away everything in the vicinity – and the crash and roar caused shock and terror even farther afield. Claudius' wife Agrippina took advantage of the emperor's alarm to accuse Narcissus, the controller of the project, of illicit profits. He retorted by assailing her dictatorial, feminine excess of ambition.

Titus celebrated the completion of the Colosseum and his neighbouring Baths by gladiatorial contests on water as well as on land. Reviving Augustus' old *naumachia* site on the Tiber's right bank (AD 80), he 'staged a sea-fight on the old artificial lake, and when the water had been let out, used the basin for further gladiatorial contests and a wild-beast hunt, 5,000 beasts of different sorts dying in a single day'. Suetonius goes straight on to make the rather strange point that 'Titus was "naturally kind-hearted" '. But there was, at any rate, no doubt about Titus' popularity, and his brother and successor Domitian was always jealous and anxious to outdo him. So he gave a sea-battle in the Colosseum itself, flooding the arena for the occasion. Domitian also had a special lake dug, 'in a new place' near the Tiber, for further nautical entertainments (AD 89). Martial went into servile raptures.

> To give a sea-fight was Augustus' care
> And rouse the waters with a trumpet's blare.
> Far greater marvels grace our monarch's reign.
> Nymphs see strange monsters rumbling in the main ...

> Caesar, such pageant as thy fertile wave
> Ne'er Amphitheatre or Circus gave.
> Prate not of Nero's pool or Fucinus.
> A true sea-battle was reserved for us.

But many events have come down to us in an anti-imperial as well as an imperial tradition. Things looked different according to whether you backed the emperor or hated him, and the Greek historian Dio Cassius, writing over a hundred years later, had inherited a less favourable account of Domitian's show. His version was that practically all the combatants perished; and so did many of the spectators as well. 'For, though a heavy rain and violent storm came up suddenly, the emperor nevertheless permitted no one to leave the spectacle; and though he himself changed his clothing to thick woollen cloaks, he would not allow the others to change their clothes, so that not a few fell sick and died. By the way, no doubt, of consoling the people for this, he provided for them at public expense a dinner all night.'

Trajan built a *naumachia Vaticana*, north-west of the future Mausoleum of Hadrian (Castel S. Angelo). In medieval times, this piece of land extending to St Peter's was known as the 'Region of the *Naumachia*'. Here or elsewhere, the emperor Philip the Arabian staged a water-battle as part of the celebrations for the millenary of Rome (AD 248).

4 THE GLADIATORS AND THEIR PUBLIC

The reputation of gladiators in the eyes of the public was curiously mixed. For one thing they were feared. Spartacus was never forgotten, and incidents that continued to occur from time to time, as well as occasional attempts to mobilize their services for uprisings and civil wars, kept these fears alive.

When the accession of Tiberius was followed by a serious mutiny among the legions on the Danube, one of the leading mutineers, Vibulenus, claimed that gladiators whom the army commander Blaesus maintained in his household were there to liquidate politically undesirable legionaries. One of their victims, he asserted, was his own brother: 'the general had him assassinated last night by the gladiators whom he keeps armed to butcher us soldiers!' Vibulenus' brother did not exist, but the fabrication shows how propagandists could play on the hysterical terrors aroused by reports of this kind. Similar alarm was no doubt caused when Gaulish professionals (*cruppellarii*) were enrolled as soldiers by Sacrovir in his national rebellion against Rome (AD 21) – though they did not fight well.

Caligula used 'Thracian' gladiators to officer his bodyguard. After his death many members of the profession flocked to the praetorian camp, and their capacity for mischief was noted again. When Claudius staged his artificial sea-battle, double companies of the praetorian guard and other units, with catapults and stone-throwers, were in attendance, stationed behind ramparts, in case the combatants got out of hand. Under Nero, panic was caused when gladiators at Praeneste (Palestrina) attempted a breakout. 'There army guards overpowered them, but the Roman public, as always terrified or fascinated by revolution, were already talking of ancient calamities such as the rising of Spartacus.'

Nor did the civil wars which followed Nero's death reassure people about the possible threat from gladiators. For, during his campaign against Vitellius, Otho recruited 2,000 of them for his army. Such men, according to Tacitus, 'were employed in the civil wars even by strict commanders; but they were an ill-favoured force to call upon'. Incidentally, this development confirmed the impression, received in Sacrovir's revolt, that a gladiator's training did not necessarily make him a good soldier, especially if he was not able to come to close grips. For in the defence of the river Po against Vitellius, Otho's recruits from the gladiators' schools did not show the normal soldierly courage of regulars. Meanwhile Vitellius had himself mobilized another gang of them, who in due course deserted to his ultimately successful enemy Vespasian. But they did not help him much, for in the confusion outside Tarracina 'a few offered resistance and inflicted some losses before they fell, but the rest of them made a rush for the ships'. Nevertheless, gladiators continued to be regarded as security risks, and this feeling no doubt revived when a member of the imperial troop participated in the assassination of Domitian.

Then again, in the grave emergency caused by German invasions, Marcus Aurelius called up not only bandits and slaves but gladiators, forming them into a unit hopefully called the 'Obedient' (*Obsequentes*). This move was badly received, not this time on grounds of public safety but because the Romans were afraid that by removing their entertainers the emperor was trying to make them turn to philosophy! Similarly, in the crisis of the civil war against Severus (AD 193), the Italy-based emperor Didius Julianus armed members of the school at Capua. Later, in the reign of Probus (276–82), eighty gladiators stationed in Rome managed to escape, and were only put down after heavy fighting.

Thus society was never able to forget for very long that the gladiators were a potential danger in its midst. So, of course, were the masses of slaves in general, and that is why their crimes were so savagely punished – if one slave murdered his master, the whole household had to die. But by their very training the gladiators offered a special peril. Moreover their legal and moral position in the community was one of utter degradation. They ranked as the lowest of the low, no better than whores, and indeed it is with male prostitutes that both Seneca and Juvenal by implication compare them. When there was a shortage of food under Augustus, the aliens and undesirables expelled from the city explicitly included the gladiators. Like members of other shameful professions and certain categories of criminal, they were *infamis* – deprived of personal dignity and outside the pale of respectable society. An inscription from Sassina or Sarsina (Mercato Saraceno) indicates the exclusion from its new cemetery of three classes of people : those who had hung themselves, those who had been engaged in immoral trades – and gladiators. When a gladiator was killed, his corpse was not permitted honourable burial, unless it was claimed by his family or owner or guild, or by a friend or admirer.

However, such claimants sometimes came forward, for inscriptions record burials by all these categories of supporter. True, when an owner of gladiators extended this attention to their dead bodies, he was sometimes acting from motives of self-advertisement. Thus certain owners have left epigraphic evidence of their own generosity in burying all the day's victims together in a single monumental tomb. This is what a certain Constantius did at Tergeste (Trieste), donating the mass grave in gratitude for having been allowed to give the games. One wonders how grateful gladiators were for a munificent act of Nero – the decoration of their biers with amber.

By way of compensation for the degraded status of the gladiators, there is ample proof of the admiration and indeed excitement that they aroused. Horace and Epictetus tell us that their doings were a staple subject of conversation. Moreover, some moved upwards into respectable smart circles of local bourgeoisies. This is clear from inscriptions at Hierapolis (Pamukkale) and Mylasa (Milas) in Asia Minor; and a retired gladiator at Ancyra (Ankara) was given honorary citizenship at no less than seven towns on either side of the Aegean. Juvenal writes of a gladiator's sons bettering themselves socially – though he does not approve of it. He is complaining of the ejection of impoverished men of respectable family from the good seats at the theatre, and he adds (whether factually, or in pursuance of a stock rhetorical theme) that among the riff-raff who shouldered them out were the offspring of gladiators.

> 'Out of the front-row seats!' they cry when you're out of money,
> Yield your place to the sons of some pimp, the spawn of some cat-house,
> Some slick auctioneer's brat, or the louts some trainer has fathered
> Or the well groomed boys whose sire is a gladiator.

A possible example of such social betterment is provided by Curtius Rufus, who was awarded a Triumph and the governorship of Africa by Claudius. The snobbish Tacitus makes heavy weather of Curtius' doubtful birth. 'Some said,' he writes, 'that he was a gladiator's son. I do not want to lie about his origin but would be embarrassed to tell the truth . . .' However, he finds it comforting to note that the man with such a background was surly though cringing to his superiors, bullying to his inferiors, and ill at ease with his equals.

But in any case, whatever might happen after retirement or in the next generation, a gladiator's career itself had its moments and aspects of glory. This impression is forcibly conveyed by innumerable representations praising gladiators and their achievements. Already in *c.* 145 BC a certain Gaius Terentius Lucanus lodged in the temple of

Diana at Aricia a painting of the contests he had paid for. Outside Pompeii, the tomb of a leading fish-paste manufacturer, Umbricius Scaurus, was adorned with stucco reliefs showing gladiatorial as well as hunting scenes; the name and school and record of each combatant is painted beside him. There are vast, unsavoury mosaics of gladiatorial fights, found at Torre Nuova near Tusculum (third century AD). Gladiators appear on further extensive mosaics from Cos, on paintings from tombs as far apart as Kertch in south Russia and north African Cyrene, and on huge numbers of lamps and gems and intaglios and funeral monuments. They are also honoured by crude pictures and inscriptions scratched on walls, for example in the Baths of Miletus and the Thracian god Azzanathkona's sanctuary at Dura-Europos in Mesopotamia.

Epigraphic references to *amatores* echo the suggestion of the poets that there was an element of homosexuality in some of this admiration; and there is a horoscope of a youth born on 6 April AD 113, Antigonus of Nicaea, who 'was erotic and fond of gladiators'. Among young women, too, in 'more than one frank outburst of rather unmaidenly admiration',[1] *graffiti* at Pompeii reveal that members of the profession were loved with the passionate infatuation which teenage females reserve for a pop singer today. Pompeian wall-inscribers called the Thracian Celadus the girls' hero and heart-throb (*suspirium et decus puellarum*); and another scrawl names the *retiarius* Crescens as the boss and healer of girls in the night (*dominum et medicum puparum nocturnarum*).

A particularly disagreeable form of erotic whimsy

1. Sir Samuel Dill.

inspired artists to represent gladiator fights between Cupids. They are seen brandishing 'Thracian' weapons in their fat hands, and a mosaic at Bignor depicts two further chubby infants engaged as *retiarius* and *secutor*.

One of Juvenal's most thundering, puritanical set-pieces deals with Eppia, who is as bad as Messalina because she eloped with a scarred, blotched, blear-eyed gladiator.

> What was the youthful charm that Eppia found so
>   enchanting?
> What did she see worth while being labelled 'The
>   Gladiatress'?
> This dear boy had begun to shave a long while ago, and one
>   arm,
> Wounded, gave hope of retirement; besides, he was fright-
>   fully ugly,
> Scarred by his helmet, a wart on his nose, and his eyes
>   always running.
> Gladiators, though, look better than any Adonis:
> This is what she preferred to children, country, and sister,
> This to her husband. The sword is what they dote on, these
>   women.

Nor was Claudius' general Curtius Rufus the only eminent man whose father, according to rumour, may have been a gladiator. Nero's adviser Nymphidius Sabinus was said to be the son of a gladiator Martianus, with whom his mother, a freedwoman, was in love. But the most conspicuous example of such gossip was the emperor Commodus, whose father was whispered to have been not Marcus Aurelius but a gladiator. This belief, however, may have been due to the son's singular tastes. For, whether his mother Faustina had this unsuitable affair or not, Commodus became unique in the sociology of Rome because, after as well as before becoming emperor, he himself engaged actively and professionally in gladiatorial combat. There had long been upper-class and even imperial amateurs; Caligula, Hadrian, Lucius Verus had all dabbled in the sport, and so did the future emperor Didius Julianus (who was criticized for going on with it too long), and the brothers Caracalla and Geta. For young men, at least, this was regarded as a suitable part-time occupation – though professional gladiators cannot altogether have enjoyed helping Caligula to practise, if it is true that 'on one occasion a fighter against whom he was fencing with a wooden sword fell down deliberately; whereupon Caligula drew a real dagger, stabbed him to death, and ran about waving the palm-branch of victory'.

But Commodus went much further, for this young emperor, according to the Greek senator, historian and eye-witness Dio Cassius, 'devoted most of his life to ease and to horses and to combats of wild beasts and men'. Before his assassination at the age of thirty-one (AD 192), he fought no less than a thousand bouts of one kind and another in the amphitheatre – 365 of them in his father's lifetime, and the rest while he himself was sole ruler. Proud of his mastery of the difficult art of left-handed fighting, he killed the animals he encountered, and none of the gladiators matched against him ventured to win. 'In fighting as a gladiator, in his own home,' Dio Cassius reported,

Commodus managed to kill a man now and then, and in making close passes with others, as if trying to clip off a bit of their hair, he sliced off the noses of some, the ears of others, and sundry features of still others. But in public he refrained from using steel and shedding human blood. Before entering the amphitheatre he would put on a long-sleeved tunic of silk, white interwoven with gold, and thus arrayed he would receive our greetings. But when he was about to go inside, he put on a robe of pure purple with gold spangles, donning also after the Greek fashion a chlamys of the same colour, and a crown made of gems from India and of gold; and he carried a herald's staff like that of Mercury. As for the lion-skin and club, in the street they were carried before him, and in the amphitheatres they were placed on a gilded chair, whether he was present or not.

This was all fuel to the flames of Commodus' passionate self-identification with Hercules, slayer of beasts and men; and it was on a statue representing himself as the god that he inscribed his claim to have overcome 12,000 opponents in the arena.

Commodus instructed that all his visits to the gladiators' school should be announced by herald. He had a room of his own there, located in the First Hall, as befitted a man who ranked, as he did, as a *secutor* of the first class. In the extravagant last year of his life, this partially deranged emperor plunged into a fourteen-day orgy of arena performances. After spending the first day shooting down a hundred bears from his platform, he settled down to a routine of slaughtering animals in the mornings and fighting as a gladiator in the afternoons. Sometimes he was accompanied in the arena by Quintus Aemilius Laetus his praetorian prefect and Eclectus the chamberlain, both of whom were already plotting his murder. 'His antagonist,' recalled Dio Cassius,

would be some athlete or perhaps a gladiator armed with a
wand. Sometimes it was a man that he himself had challenged,
sometimes one chosen by the people. For in this as well as other
matters he put himself on an equal footing with the other
gladiators – except for the fact that they enter the lists for a
very small sum, whereas Commodus received a million sesterces
from the gladiatorial fund each day. And when he had finished
his sparring match, and of course won it, he would then, just as
he was, kiss his companions (Laetus and Eclectus) through his
helmet.

After this the regular contestants would fight. The first day
Commodus personally paired all the combatants down in the
arena, where he appeared with all the trappings of Hermes
(Mercury), including a gilded wand, and took his place on a
gilded platform; and we regarded his doing this as an omen.
Later he would ascend to his customary place and from there
view the remainder of the spectacle with us. After that the contests no longer resembled child's play, but were so serious that
great numbers of men were killed.

When the emperor was fighting, we senators together with
the knights always attended ... we would shout out whatever
we were commanded, and especially these words continually :
*Thou art lord and thou art first! Of all men most fortunate!
Victor thou art! And victor thou shalt be! From everlasting,
Amazonian, thou art victor.*

Faced, on one occasion, by the emperor brandishing with a
leer the severed head of an ostrich, Dio Cassius and his
friends only prevented themselves from giving way to
nervous laughter – which might have had fatal results – by
plucking laurel leaves from their garlands and chewing them
so as to keep their jaws occupied.

If Commodus had survived just one more day, he would

have entered his consulship at the New Year of AD 193 in the uniform of a *secutor*. But this sort of prospect was too much for his advisers and his mistress, who sent an athlete called Narcissus to strangle him in his bath.

The profession could not boast of an emperor-gladiator every day.[2] Yet, even if they were not emperors, there is also evidence from many epochs indicating that even the rank and file of gladiators, amid the ruthless conditions of their employment, maintained some pride and communal spirit. When Tiberius was economizing on gladiatorial shows, Seneca the younger heard of a *myrmillo* complaining that his time was being wasted; some imperial gladiators were angry if they were not given a chance to fight. Keen supporters of the games argued, like defenders of fox-hunting or bull-fighting, that the participants enjoyed them as much as the spectators.

They were pleased enough with themselves to assume grandiose professional names, associated with victory or with heroic mythology. Moreover, certain of them were too proud to fight except with those of equal status to themselves. Out of this same pride, or perhaps partly from the Roman passion for organization, gladiators were formed into an elaborate hierarchy, rising at the top of each branch to the rank of *primus palus* or first-class fighter. Every school, and every branch of the profession within a school, had its first, second, third and fourth grades, and these were accommodated in separate Halls.

2. Though the *Historia Augusta* quoted a rumour that another emperor, Macrinus (217–18), had been a gladiator in earlier life.

The lives of gladiators were mostly all too brutally short. A typical epitaph tells of one who met his end at the age of twenty-two after five fights, in the sixth year of his marriage. Yet it was possible for a slave who was a gladiator to survive, win liberation, and retire, on receipt of the symbolical wooden sword (*rudis*). There was sometimes an element of caprice in the selection of these *rudiarii*. According to Suetonius, 'when four brothers pleaded for the discharge of their father, a chariot-fighter, Claudius presented him with the customary wooden sword amid resounding cheers, and then wrote a note for the herald to read aloud: "You now see the great advantage of having a large family; it can win favour and protection even for a gladiator." ' The epitaph of a first-class ex-fighter (*summus rudiarius*) shows that he survived to the age of sixty. Such veterans of the first and second grade were employed by gladiatorial schools as overseers and inspectors. A Syrian fighter, Flamma, received the wooden sword four times and each time signed on again. It was possible to resume one's engagement either for the school or for combat or both.

A strong *esprit de corps* was shown by some of Commodus' gladiators who formed a guild of their own; and this too was hierarchically organized. The primary purpose of the Commodus group was to honour the god Silvanus. Among other deities to whom gladiators showed especial corporate and individual devotion were Mars, Diana and above all Hercules. There was also keen attention to Victoria, Fortuna and Nemesis – though one epitaph warns other fighters not to trust her protection.

Another such memorial, from Smyrna (Izmir), tells how

a whole troop contributed to the funeral of the little child of one of their colleagues. Similar fellow-feeling is shown by the tomb of a *retiarius* of the Great School at Rome, put up by a *myrmillo* who was his mess-mate; and a *secutor* is likewise presented with his gravestone by a colleague. The whole 'Thracian' group (*armatura*) perform the same service for one of their number, and Crispus, a gladiator of the type known as *provocator*, is similarly honoured by his compatriots.

A papyrus has preserved this tragic *cri de coeur* from a woman who had lost her gladiator lover:

> At the command of a proud man, *myrmillo*
> Among the net fighters, alas you are gone,
> Gripping in strong hands a sword your sole weapon,
> And me you have left in my anguish alone.

Many epitaphs of fallen fighters strike the same note; some were defrayed by their fans (*amatores*), but most by their widows. Often, too, there is a pretence that they were written by the combatants themselves, who are rather naïvely made to testify to their own strength and endurance, generosity and lack of malice, and good temper. As on the accompanying reliefs which display them fighting or triumphant, the prevailing sentiment is glory, but there are many tragic undercurrents.

> 'Killed not by man but fate'
> 'Won but died of wounds'
> 'Avenged by my comrade'

'Loved by everyone'
'No one suffered from me, but now I suffer'
'Spared many lives'.

Such are the men whom the poet Martial salutes in the person of the successful, chivalrous fighter Hermes.

Hermes, merciful to vanquished foes,
Hermes, who no understudy knows ...
Hermes, miracle of record-breaking,
Hermes, past comparing or mistaking!

When Byron says of the Colosseum, 'Heroes have trod this spot,' he is speaking of Christian martyrs, and the courage of the martyrs was a noble thing which came out of that dreadful place. But so was the pathetic individual bravery of millions of gladiators throughout the centuries. This bravery deeply impressed Cicero, who asked why, if such outcasts from society can act so courageously, the rest of us cannot behave better than we do.

Look at gladiators, who are either ruined men or barbarians, what blows they endure! See how men, who have been well trained, prefer to receive a blow rather than basely avoid it! How frequently it is made evident that there is nothing they put higher than giving satisfaction to their owner or to the people! Even when weakened with wounds they send word to their owners to ascertain their pleasure: if they have given satisfaction to them they are content to fall. What gladiator of ordinary merit has ever uttered a groan or changed countenance? Who of them has disgraced himself, I will not say upon his feet, but who has disgraced himself in his fall? Who after falling has drawn in his neck when ordered to suffer the fatal stroke? Such is the force of training, practice and habit. Shall then the Samnite, filthy fellow, worthy of his life and place, be capable of this, and shall a man born to fame have any portion of his soul so weak that he cannot strengthen it by systematic preparation?

The Augustan historian Dionysius of Halicarnassus like-wise expressed amazement at what gladiators were pre-pared to go through in order to win their crown. The valour they continually showed in the arena was all the more wonderful because of the unspeakable sufferings they knew and saw at the closest quarters. Seeing comrades mutilated and struck down makes steadfast endurance that much harder, and the slaughter that preceded one's own fight must have undermined the toughest morale. Nor can their heroism be dismissed as a mere brutalized insensitive-ness. The humanity of many a gladiator's epitaph tells a very different story.

THE ATTITUDES OF RULERS AND SPECTATORS

Gladiatorial duels had originated from funeral games given in order to satisfy the dead man's need for blood; and for centuries their principal occasions were funerals. Accord-ingly a religious aura continued to hang about such con-tests – if only in the eyes of educated traditionalists.

There were other motives, too, which inspired the Roman ruling classes to view these contests with a favour-able eye. The ancient excuse of encouragement to warlike toughness continued to be put forward until the eve of the Middle Ages, although it came to sound increasingly lame and inhumane. Another purpose present in the minds of Rome's rulers was the desire that the potentially unruly and dangerous city population should be amused and kept quiet, by being given the entertainment that they wanted, however repulsive it might be.

Indeed, the principal attraction of such combats was this very nastiness. The Romans' enjoyment of the sport was horrifyingly brutal and perverted. If this needs documenting, we can direct a glance or two at the imperial platform, since its occupants' reactions were seen and have consequently come down to us. There we can note the embarrassingly keen interest in bloodshed displayed by Tiberius' son Drusus; or the macabre unpleasantnesses of Caligula.

During gladiatorial shows, says Suetonius, this emperor 'would have the canopies removed at the hottest time of the day and forbid anyone to leave; or cancel the regular programme, and pit feeble old fighters against decrepit criminals; or stage comic duels between respectable householders, who happened to be physically disabled in some way or other.'

Moreover, cruelty was blended with jealousy. Aesius Proculus, a leading centurion's son, was so good-looking that he was nicknamed 'Giant Cupid'. So Caligula had him dragged from his seat and matched with a *retiarius* and then a *secutor*. Proculus won both times, but was paraded through the streets in rags and then executed.

Some of these incidents might be fictitious, but not all; and they were not isolated. There can be no very pleasant diagnosis of the next emperor Claudius, if he really ordered that fallen fighters, especially *retiarii*, should have their

throats cut so that he could watch their faces as they died.
Likewise Domitian, amid hilarious laughter from his court-
poets, set not only women but dwarfs and cripples fighting.
The imperial gladiator Commodus carried cruelty to even
greater lengths. 'Once,' recorded Dio Cassius, 'he got together all the men in the city who had lost their feet as
the result of disease or some accident, and then, after fast-
ening about their knees some likenesses of serpents' bodies,
and giving them sponges to throw instead of stones, killed
them with blows of a club, pretending that they were
giants' – a strange piece of mythological beastliness,
symbolizing the emperor's divine role as Herculean ex-
terminator of monsters. After that his treatment of
fellow-gladiators seems almost straightforward. 'On one
occasion, when some of the victors hesitated to slay the vanquished, he fastened the various contestants together and
ordered them all to fight at once. Thereupon the men so
bound fought man against man, and some killed even
those who did not belong to their group at all, since the
numbers and the limited space had brought them together.'

If rulers of the empire committed such detestable extrava-
gances, the reactions of other spectators were unlikely to be
any more high-minded. Many of them, it is true, must also
have been capable of appreciating the finer technical points
of combat. But nearly all of them also wallowed unrestrain-
edly in blood-lust. Petronius' Echion entertains high hopes
of a forthcoming display, because its patron 'will give us
cold steel, no quarter and the slaughterhouse right in the
middle where all the stands can see it'. And nothing can
be more frank than the Minturnae inscription on which

Publius Baebius Justus – in connection, as it happens, with a slaughter not of gladiators but of ten bears – is explicitly credited with having these animals killed CRVDEL*iter* – cruelly. The word is apparently inserted as an expression of praise! More cruelty was openly equated with more fun.

The constant recurrence of this unrestrained blood-thirstiness throughout long centuries is one of the most appalling manifestations of evil that the world has ever known. The reactions of spectators unmistakably assumed that form of perverted sexuality known as sadism – which is likewise a major feature of our own modern community. Occasional sadistic murders shock and alarm the public, and blood-sports are accused of ill-effects on some of their participants, but the principal manifestation of the tend-ency is cheap literature incorporating sadistic fantasies and their masochistic counterparts. Other societies have operated different safety-valves. The Spanish taste for ex-citement and blood finds its outlet in bull-fighting; the Nazis slaughtered human beings on a scale exceeding even that of the Romans.

Our knowledge of the correlation between literary or visual sadistic entertainments, crimes of violence, and social conditions, is still rudimentary. Schopenhauer be-lieved that man outdoes the tiger and hyena in pitiless cruelty, and Sigmund Freud, seeing sadism and masochism as innate, evolved several different theories regarding the impulses which make men 'savage beasts to whom the thought of sparing their kind is alien'. Against this, Karen Horney cited the Arapesh tribe of New Guinea and the Zuni of New Mexico, in whom the nastier tendencies seem to be lacking. But now Konrad Lorenz has argued that, although by nature man was not very aggressive, his discovery of weapons long since provided a terrible substitute for his natural lack of animal rage.

Freud's associate and rival Wilhelm Stekel maintained, like him, that 'in the human soul cruelty lies, like a beast, chained, but eager to spring'. In studying the subject, he turned his attention to the gladiators of ancient Rome, seeing the institution as an expression of hatred and the will to power – a part of those qualities in the Romans which also led to their conquests (and the *pax Romana*). And it is true that conquering powers exhibit crude or aggressive sporting tastes. But this hardly accounts, in itself, for the intense, continuous carnage and blood-lust of the arena. Moreover, as Otto Kiefer points out in his study of Roman sexuality, it is not accurate to look only at the proliferation of *later* imperial bestialities, and then to claim that they were the sign of a degenerate society. On the contrary, they had been present from very early times, for example in an abundance of tortures and floggings, and in execution customs so repellent that they have had to be ascribed to the victim's ritual representation of a sacrificial animal. These were not late degenerate horrors but early, endemic, and never far from the surface.

Another factor to be reckoned with was the absolute mastery of the early Roman paterfamilias over his children. 'The Roman lawgiver,' wrote Dionysius of Halicarnassus, 'gave the father complete power over the son, power which lasted a whole lifetime. He was at liberty to imprison him, flog him, to keep him a prisoner working on the farm, and to kill him.' And though the laws were modified, much of the spirit remained. Psychoanalysts have shown how aggression in parents causes sadism to develop later in their children. Moreover the sadist, like the fire-raiser or the lyncher, relieves his own latent fears by doing to another what he fears might be done to him.[3] For the Roman was not only brutalized in childhood, but lived in a society where violence might easily descend upon him. Other peoples have started with similar savageries, but have managed to grow out of them; the Romans disastrously failed to do so, instead allowing the worst of such manifestations, gladiatorial combat, to become a vast and permanent and officially sponsored institution.

As Freud's successors shifted the emphasis from biological to sociological and cultural factors, universal aggression and brutality were attributed to frustration, disastrous social conditions, and the 'failure to obtain love'.[4]

Erich Fromm's view of sadism as one of the things that arise from unconscious attempts to escape from intolerable helpless isolation has a bearing on the Roman predicament. Already earlier, when the parochial Greek city-states had been absorbed or eclipsed by huge Hellenistic kingdoms, the resultant lonely defencelessness of the individual had created a widespread 'collapse of nerve'. In the vast Roman world these symptoms became accentuated, permanent and ubiquitous. Millions of people felt shiftless, unsupported, un-looked after, lost – and above all bored.

The plunge into religion was one compensatory reaction. But another was immersion in sanguinary sadism. Religion

3. Aggression of parents: L. Bender, F. J. Curran. Relief of fears: B. Karpman.

4. J. F. Brown; Wilhelm Reich; Karen Horney.

had its share of this, notably in the ghastly drenchings in bull's blood which comprised the very popular pagan baptism rite known as the *taurobolium*. But nothing could touch the gladiatorial combats for excitement. And into these plunged the millions of Rome's citizens and subjects all the more keenly because they were encouraged to adopt this outlet by their rulers, as an apparently inconsiderable evil, or no evil at all, in comparison with the political insecurity and sedition which might result from the absence of such distractions.

THE ATTITUDES OF WRITERS

The attitude of many Romans, even men of the highest culture, towards the arena was flawed and inhumane – or, if disapproving, not disapproving enough. Cicero says people are bored by excess of gladiatorial shows. 'This type of display', he remarks, 'is apt to seem cruel and brutal to some eyes, and I incline to think that it is so, as now conducted. But in the days when it was criminals who crossed swords in the death struggle, there could be no better schooling against pain and death – at any rate for the eye, though for the ear perhaps there might be many.' The suggestion, then, is that the combats have deteriorated and become unproductive of pleasure but that they were originally a noble and educational art – good virile training, as the rulers of the Republic had thought. This is typical of a certain equivocation in Cicero who, although steeped in Greek culture, often criticized its anti-Roman softness, partly for appearance's sake but partly because of a genuine ambivalence.

A century and a half later, Pliny the younger is equally

disappointing. He praises a friend who gave a gladiatorial display, and approves of the disdain of death and love of honourable wounds which such combats encouraged, inspiring, he said, ambition in the hearts even of criminals and slaves. Nowhere do we see more clearly than in the inadequate comments of this usually kind-hearted man what it was to live in a society where some people had no rights at all; and where policy and tradition had institutionalized the brutalities inherent in this situation.

Equally unattractive, at the very end of antiquity and in a time of growing Christian humanitarianism, is the attitude of the highly educated pagan Symmachus. Reference has been made to the heart-rending incident when twenty-nine Saxon prisoners of war succeeded in strangling one another rather than fight duels in Symmachus' games. But his comment is merely this: 'evidently no guard, however efficient, can restrain that desperate race'. The climate of opinion still encouraged Constantine the Great, the first Christian emperor, to throw masses of German prisoners (Bructeri) into the arena and have them torn to pieces by wild animals – the fate that Christians had suffered for centuries. The comment of his cultured panegyrists is that he 'delighted the people with the wholesale annihilation of their enemies – and what triumph could have been finer?'

On the other hand, from the time of the early principate onwards, the rhetorical schools which comprised Rome's higher educational system had been building up a series of stock themes criticizing the barbarities of gladiatorial combats. The practical effect of these objections was slight or non-existent. Yet it is important that they were voiced; and

they were translated into significant literary denunciations.
The earliest and most notable protest comes from the
Romano-Spanish philosopher, essayist and dramatist Seneca
the younger. Whatever his equivocations as Nero's minis-
ter, he must be credited with the first known unambiguous
attack upon the whole institution of gladiators, and the
popular enjoyment of its human bloodshed. Seneca invokes
the Stoic Universal Brotherhood. 'Man,' he asserts, 'is a
thing which is sacred to mankind. But nowadays he is killed
in play, for fun! It was once a sin to teach him how to
inflict wounds or receive them. But now he is led out naked
and defenceless – and provides a sufficient show by his
death.'

He illustrates his hatred of such vileness from a certain
sort of combat which was timed for the hour of midday.
The fighters sent into the arena in this slack period were
unpractised and almost undefending victims; this was an
entr'acte of sheer massacre.

By chance I attended a midday exhibition, expecting some
fun, wit, and relaxation – an exhibition at which men's eyes
have respite from the slaughter of their fellow-men. But it was
quite the reverse. The previous combats were the essence of
compassion; but now all the trifling is put aside and it is pure
murder. The men have no defensive armour. They are exposed to
blows at all points, and no one ever strikes in vain. Many
persons prefer this programme to the usual pairs and to the
bouts 'by request'. Of course they do; there is no helmet or
shield to deflect the weapon. What is the need of defensive
armour, or of skill? All these mean delaying death. In the morning they throw men to the lions and the bears: at noon, they
throw them to the spectators. The spectators demand that the

slayer shall face the man who is to slay him in his turn; and they always reserve the latest conqueror for another butchering. The outcome of every fight is death, and the means are fire and sword. This sort of thing goes on while the arena is empty.

You may retort: 'But he was a highway robber; he killed a man!' And what of it? Granted that, as a murderer, he deserved this punishment, what crime have you committed, poor fellow, that you should deserve to sit and see this show? In the morning they cried 'Kill him! Lash him! Burn him! Why does he meet the sword in so cowardly a way? Why does he strike so feebly? Why doesn't he die game? Whip him to meet his wounds! Let them receive blow for blow, with chests bare and exposed to the stroke!' And when the games stop for the intermission, they announce: 'A little throat-cutting in the meantime, so that there may still be something going on!'

And Seneca's comment on this abomination is that 'nothing is so damaging to good character as the habit of lounging at the games, for then it is that vice steals subtly upon one through the avenue of pleasure. What do you think I mean? I mean that I come home more greedy, more ambitious, more voluptuous, and even more cruel and inhuman – because I have been among human beings.'

Such an appeal against this degradation of the human spirit was a mere drop in the ocean of universal savagery fomented by official support. Yet there were other philosophers and thinkers of the imperial epoch, Greeks and orientals rather than Romans, who spoke out as uncompromisingly as Seneca. Artemidorus of Daldis, whose interpretation of dreams was mentioned at the beginning of this study, described the gladiators' profession as a dishonourable, cruel and impious career founded on human blood.

He was probably a Stoic like Seneca; and the far greater Stoic Epictetus, a crippled Phrygian slave, was likewise nauseated by the whole business[5] – writing with bitter irony of the elegant high priest who takes meticulous care of his fine gladiatorial troop in which he has invested.

Similar sentiments were uttered by other Greek and Hellenized philosophers of the second century AD. To Dio Chrysostom of Prusa these duels are *the unspeakable thing*. Plutarch recommends towns to abolish their fights, or at least to limit and hamper them. That fearless critic Lucian writes of gladiators' combats in his *Anacharsis*, where a speaker condemns them as bestial, crude, harmful, and destructive of material that would be useful against Rome's enemies. In Lucian's *Demonax* the same note is struck, for when the Athenians of these Roman imperial times were thinking, in their rivalry with Corinth, of starting gladiatorial shows, we are told how the philosopher Demonax came forward and said, 'Men of Athens, before you pass this motion, do not forget to destroy the Altar of Pity.' And we hear from Dionysius of another philosopher who was driven into exile for taking the same unpopular line.

But the most explicit condemnation of all comes from an unidentifiable follower of the ancient school of Pythagoras, whose work *On the Eating of Flesh*, written in imperial times, contains a warning even more specific than Seneca's about the moral corruption with which a taste for gladiator shows infects the spectators. For these results are correctly defined by the anonymous Neo-Pythagorean as 'insensibility to human beings, and cruelty'.

5. Though in un-Greek fashion he takes the same view of athletes!

Such were the few and scattered voices that protested against the destructive effects of this never-ending flow of gladiatorial slaughter upon the watching crowds. But the objectors could not fail to receive adherents from among the rapidly increasing Christians, whose doctrines both respected human life and paid attention to the lost and oppressed. In about AD 200 the fiery anti-pagan eloquence of the African Tertullian is devoted to this theme, with particular reference to the infamous custom or pretence that death in the arena was regarded as a justifiable punishment for crime.

He who shudders at the body of a man who died by nature's law the common death of all, will, in the amphitheatre, gaze down with most tolerant eyes on the bodies of men mangled, torn in pieces, defiled with their own blood; yes, and he who comes to the spectacle to signify his approval of murder being punished, will have a reluctant gladiator hounded on with lash and rod to do murder . . .

If we can plead that cruelty is allowed us, if impiety, if brute savagery, by all means let us go to the amphitheatre. If we are what people say we are, let us take our delight in the blood of men. 'It is a good thing, when the guilty are punished.' Who will deny that, unless he is one of the guilty? And yet the innocent cannot take pleasure in the punishment of another, when it better befits the innocent to lament that a man like himself has become so guilty that a punishment so cruel must be awarded him.

But it remained for Augustine, writing in his *Confessions* nearly two hundred years later, to depict in final and unforgettable terms (echoed by Mérimée on Spanish bull-fighting) the dreadful fascination which gladiatorial bestialities had exerted upon a previously innocent spectator, his young friend Alypius.

He had gone to Rome before me in order to study law, and in Rome he had been quite swept away, incredibly and with a most incredible passion, by the gladiatorial shows. He was opposed to such things and detested them; but he happened to meet some of his friends and fellow pupils on their way back from dinner, and they, in spite of his protests and his vigorous resistance, used a friendly kind of violence and forced him to go along with them to the amphitheatre on a day when one of those cruel and bloody shows was being presented. As he went, he said to them: 'You can drag my body there, but don't imagine that you can make me turn my eyes or give my mind to the show. Though there, I shall not be there, and so I shall have the better both of you and of the show.'

After hearing this his friends were all the keener to bring him along with them. No doubt they wanted to see whether he could actually do this or not. So they came to the arena and took the seats which they could find. The whole place was seething with savage enthusiasm, but he shut the doors of his eyes and forbade his soul to go out into a scene of such evil. If only he could have blocked up his ears too! For in the course of the fight some man fell; there was a great roar from the whole mass of spectators which fell upon his ears; he was overcome by curiosity and opened his eyes, feeling perfectly prepared to treat whatever he might see with scorn and to rise above it.

But he then received in his soul a worse wound than that man, whom he had wanted to see, had received in his body. His own fall was more wretched than that of the gladiator which had caused all that shouting which had entered his ears and unlocked his eyes and made an opening for the thrust which was to overthrow his soul – a soul that had been reckless rather than strong and was all the weaker because it had trusted in itself when it ought to have trusted in You. He saw the blood and he gulped down savagery. Far from turning away, he fixed his eyes on it. Without knowing what was happening, he drank in madness, he was delighted with the guilty contest, drunk with the lust of blood. He was no longer the man who had come there but was one of the crowd to which he had come, a true companion of those who had brought him.

There is no more to be said. He looked, he shouted, he raved with excitement. He took away with him a madness which would goad him to come back again, and he would not only come with those who first got him there; he would go ahead of them and he would drag others with him . . .

But it must not be thought that the anguished reproaches of the *Confessions* were particularly typical of that time, or even later. The cold-blooded remarks of Constantine's panegyrist and Symmachus have been quoted; and Augustine's other contemporary Libanius, the fine flower of classical culture and Hellenism, admitted to a special love for the combats of gladiators, whom he regarded as 'disciples of the heroes of Thermopylae' (later, however, he reversed this opinion).

THE ABOLITION OF THE GLADIATORS

Although Constantine the Great made many a German prisoner fight in the arena, he later issued from Berytus (Beirut) an edict ostensibly abolishing gladiators' games altogether (AD 326). This initiative may have been due to pressure from the Fathers of the Church assembled for the Nicaean Council. The edict added that all criminals who would in the past have been enrolled for the games must in future be condemned to forced labour in the mines instead. This portion of the order was probably put into effect (though, owing to desperate conditions in the mines, it may not have been welcomed by victims), but the main prohibition was not enforced, at least in Italy. Indeed there it was very soon denied by Constantine himself, when he wrote to the town of Hispellum (Spello) agreeing that municipal priests in Umbria should continue to give gladiators' shows, and that their colleagues in Etruscan towns should combine forces in this respect so as to concentrate their displays at Etruria's religious centre of Volsinii (Orvieto). The December games given by the quaestors at Rome still figure in a list of annual festivals belonging to the year AD 354, the Calendar of Philocalus. The Church had ruled that gladiators and their trainers, and people concerned with gladiatorial displays and wild-beast shows, were ineligible for baptism. But the declaration of Christianity as the official religion of the empire did not at first put a stop to gladiatorial combats.

Yet restrictive legislation was again on the way. An edict of Constantius II (357) forbade soldiers and officials in Rome to take part personally in the games, penalizing those who did so, and eight and again ten years later Valentinian I prohibited the condemnation of Christians to the gladiators' schools: from which moreover, before long, no senators were allowed to accept an inmate in their household (397). Five years earlier St John Chrysostom was still referring to gladiatorial performances at Antioch – perhaps almost the last to take place in an eastern province. At Rome, in 399, the western emperor Honorius closed what remained of the gladiatorial schools. Even so, however, the date when the institution ceased to exist had apparently not quite arrived. When Augustine in the *Confessions* (*c.* 400) told of his friend's seduction by the arena, it did not sound as if the danger was dead, and two or three years later the poet Prudentius, in his denunciation of the pagan Symmachus, was still urging the emperor to forbid the use of such shows in order to inflict death-sentences upon criminals. Curiously enough, Prudentius suggested that the emperor should instead only allow them to be pitted against wild beasts – a sport which still persisted, although the state was now Christian. In the eastern empire the puritan, economical ruler Anastasius I seems, in 498, to have forbidden contests of men against wild beasts, but to have still allowed wild beasts to be pitted against one another. In Italy, after the western emperors had come to an end, the Ostrogothic ruler Theoderic (493–526) may have passed a similar enactment, for he is reported by Cassiodorus to have denounced a performance in 523. Final abolition seems to have come in 681.

As regards gladiators, however, Prudentius' plea was said to have been followed by a critical event. This, if the story is true, was precipitated by Telemachus (also known as St Almachius) a monk from Asia Minor, who rushed into a Roman arena to part the fighters, and was torn to pieces by the infuriated crowd. Honorius seized the opportunity to abolish gladiators and their games altogether. This event is usually dated to AD 404. Some have argued that a similar incident took place in 392, and that this date is to be preferred to 404. But gladiatorial exhibitions did not end in 392, though gladiatorial schools closed at about this time. Indeed, the combats did not finish in 404 either; perhaps they continued as late as 439–40.

As a consolation to those horrified by the gladiators, it has been suggested that these orgies of cruelty were bound to produce the Christian Gospel of Love to counteract and in the end abolish them; and that the games accordingly provide one of the reasons why Christianity conquered the Roman empire. This is a somewhat two-edged argument. It is true that humanitarian tendencies already evident in pagan Rome – notably in the writings of its great lawyers – could not fail to find intenser expression in the Christian doctrines which exercised so wide an appeal because of their emphasis upon the humble and distressed. Indeed, this change is reflected in the denunciations of gladiators by Christians such as Tertullian and Augustine. Yet other very forcible onslaughts upon the institution had already come much earlier from pagans including Seneca and Greek or Hellenized writers. Moreover, some of the most bloodthirsty human holocausts in the arena were perpetrated by Constantine the Great, who made the empire officially Christian; and gladiatorial combats were not abolished until a hundred years, or much more, after the Christian revelation that he claimed to have experienced. Yet, for all that, it was appropriate that a monk should have taken the initiative in the final abolition of this scandal. For in the last resort, and in spite of the long time-lag, its termination must be attributed to the spreading of Christian ideas. They did not, it is true, limit other forms of carnage in the Roman world. Even massacres of, and by, wild beasts continued for a long time; persecution flourished; and the other cruelties and miseries of ancient life did not diminish. Yet those who believed in the Gospel of Christ could not, and did not, for ever tolerate the fighting of gladiators for public entertainment.

NOTES ON
FURTHER READING

There are valuable collections of material about gladiators in the following books :

J. P. V. D. Balsdon, *Life and Leisure in Ancient Rome*, Bodley Head, 1969, pp. 288–302.

M. Brion, *La Révolte des Gladiateurs*, Paris, 1952.

J. Carcopino, *Daily Life in Ancient Rome*, Penguin ed., 1956.

D. Faccenna, *Rilievi di Gladiatori*, in *Bull. della Comm. Arch. Com. di Roma*, 1956–8, pp. 55–8.

L. Friedländer-Drexel, *Darstellungen aus der Sittengeschichte Roms*, 10th edition, 1920 (there is an English translation of the 7th edition entitled *Roman Life and Manners under the Early Empire*).

G. Lafaye, in C. Daremberg and E. Saglio, *Dictionnaire des antiquités grecques et romaines*, Vol. II, pp. 1563–99.

J. H. Oliver and R. E. A. Palmer, *Minutes of an Act of the Roman Senate*, 'Hesperia', 24, 1955, pp. 320ff.

A. Piganiol, *Les Trinci gaulois: gladiateurs consacrés*, 'Revue des Etudes Anciennes', 20, 1922, pp. 283ff.

T. Rice Holmes, *The Roman Republic*, O.U.P., 1923, pp. 156–61, 386–90 (Spartacus).

L. Robert, *Gladiateurs dans l'Orient Grec*, Paris, 1940.

E. T. Salmon, *Samnium and the Samnites*, Cambridge, 1967, pp. 60ff.

K. Schneider, in Pauly-Wissowa-Kroll, *Real-Encyclopädie der Classischen Altertumswissenschaft*, Suppl. Vol. III, 1918, columns 760–84.

G. Ville, *La Mosaïque gréco-romaine*, Paris, 1963, pp. 147ff.

G. Ville, *Les Jeux de gladiateurs dans l'empire chrétien*, in *Mélanges d'archéologie et d'histoire*, 1960, pp. 273–335.

INDEX